Put Y

Praise for *Put Your Mindset to Work*:

'The insights in this book could have saved me and any top employer a lot of elementary mistakes, never mind the additional cost of bad decisions'
Gordon Roddick, co-founder, The Body Shop

'*Put Your Mindset to Work* changes the conversation when it comes to recruitment and selection. Everyone wants the winning mindset. This great book tells you what it looks like and how to make the most of it'
John Ayton, co-founder, Links of London

'A hugely informative and enjoyable book, [filled with] practical, easy-to use tools. The case studies are inspiring'
Simon Lloyd, HR director, Santander UK

'The 3G Mindset will give you new insight and understanding into what it really takes to succeed. A good read that provides thought-provoking and practical advice for all those developing their careers'
Andy Doyle, group HR director, ITV Group

'This book provides the definitive answer for anyone trying to gauge, strengthen, and apply mindset to gain a powerful edge'
Stephen Burrill, Deloitte

'What if the key to handling the most complex leadership and talent management challenges hinged on the very way you think? Reed and Stoltz provide a powerful model and toolkit [to get] exceptional results'
Joshua Margolis, Harvard Business School

'*Put Your Mindset to Work* provides practical and insightful strategies for assessing and developing organizational talent. A groundbreaking look at how to leverage your mindset to create an advantage in the marketplace'
Tamar Elkeles, Qualcomm

'The knowledge and concepts conveyed in this book are critical elements in the hiring equation. This book is a resource to any organization or leader who wants to recruit and retain top talent'
Chris Powell, Scripps Networks Interactive

'James Reed and Paul Stoltz dare to assert that skills guarantee nothing and that it takes more than guts to succeed – it's mindset that trumps everything. They back up this truth with real-life examples and impressive research on what really counts in getting the best jobs, reaching your earning potential, and flourishing beyond work'
Jim Kouzes, co-author of the bestselling *The Leadership Challenge* and *The Truth about Leadership*

'This book marries rock-solid science with compelling tools to provide the definitive solution to landing, keeping, and thriving in the best jobs. This one goes front and centre on my bookshelf'
Harry Hoopis, chairman, Hoopis Financial Services

'If you want a book that equips you to stand out from the crowd and become immensely desirable to the best companies, get *Put Your Mindset to Work!*'
Christi Strauss, president and CEO, Cereal Partners Worldwide

ABOUT THE AUTHORS

James Reed is the chairman of REED, the recruitment specialist which places hundreds of thousands of people into roles around the world every year. James Reed joined the company in 1991 after graduating from Harvard Business School. In the twenty years since then REED has more than quadrupled in size, while reed.co.uk has become the number one job site in the UK and Europe. REED now receives more than 20 million job applications a year, and has helped more than 100,000 long-term unemployed people get back into work. James Reed is also a fellow of the Chartered Institute of Personnel and Development (CIPD). He lives with his wife and family in London.

Paul Stoltz is the world's leading expert on measuring and strengthening human resilience. He is the author of three bestselling books, printed in fifteen languages. In 1987 Dr Stoltz founded PEAK Learning, a research and consulting firm, through which he coaches and collaborates with leaders and influencers across a range of organizations. He has been honoured as 'Thought Leader of the Year' and 'One of the 100 Most Influential Thinkers of Our Time' (Executive Excellence). PEAK Learning's headquarters is perched on a cattle ranch in the foothills of the central coast of California, where Dr Stoltz resides with his family.

Put Your Mindset to Work

THE ONE ASSET YOU REALLY NEED TO WIN AND KEEP THE JOB YOU LOVE

James Reed and Paul G. Stoltz, PhD

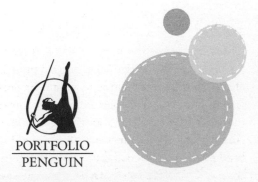

PORTFOLIO
PENGUIN

PORTFOLIO PENGUIN

Published by the Penguin Group
Penguin Books Ltd, 80 Strand, London WC2R 0RL, England
Penguin Group (USA) Inc., 375 Hudson Street, New York, New York 10014, USA
Penguin Group (Canada), 90 Eglinton Avenue East, Suite 700, Toronto,
Ontario, Canada M4P 2Y3 (a division of Pearson Penguin Canada Inc.)
Penguin Ireland, 25 St Stephen's Green, Dublin 2, Ireland
(a division of Penguin Books Ltd)
Penguin Group (Australia), 250 Camberwell Road,Camberwell, Victoria 3124, Australia
(a division of Pearson Australia Group Pty Ltd)
Penguin Books India Pvt Ltd, 11 Community Centre, Panchsheel Park,
New Delhi – 110 017, India
Penguin Group (NZ), 67 Apollo Drive, Rosedale, Auckland 0632, New Zealand
(a division of Pearson New Zealand Ltd)
Penguin Books (South Africa) (Pty) Ltd, 24 Sturdee Avenue, Rosebank,
Johannesburg 2196, South Africa

Penguin Books Ltd, Registered Offices: 80 Strand, London WC2R 0RL, England

www.penguin.com

First published in the United States of America by Portfolio/Penguin,
a member of Penguin Group (USA) Inc. 2011
First published in Great Britain by Portfolio Penguin 2011

1

Printed in Great Britain by Clays Ltd, St Ives plc

A CIP catalogue record for this book is available from the British Library

ISBN: 978–0–670–92051–8

www.greenpenguin.co.uk

Penguin Books is committed to a sustainable
future for our business, our readers and our
planet. This book is made from paper certified
by the Forest Stewardship Council.

This book is dedicated to all
who seek to make work more than a job.

CONTENTS

Put Your
Mindset to Work

WHY MINDSET MATTERS

The promise this book makes to you is simple: you can multiply your chances of getting the job you want and enjoy uncommon success at work while enriching your life immensely along the way.

Our promise is grounded in the surprising truth about what employers *really* want along with the rigorous scientific research and proven results of our years in the real world of business. We back up our promise and every claim we make in this book with evidence. No hype. That's part of our promise too.

You can immediately apply the new tools and ideas we provide throughout to:

- Triple your chances of getting and keeping the best job
- Achieve seven times the value of a "normal employee" in the eyes of your boss or key stakeholders
- Measurably enhance your earning potential
- Be promoted over other, supposedly more "qualified" candidates
- Create genuine job security by becoming the last person any employer would let go, even when job cuts are severe

- Earn top performance ratings from even the toughest boss or stakeholders
- Flourish at and beyond work, at any stage in the game

And that's just for starters. All you need is the right mindset.

The Beginning – The Double Wake-up Call

This book is a collaborative effort that started when both authors experienced their own wake-up calls about what actually makes for a successful career. Our realizations relate to every worker, every applicant and every employer. They are wake-up calls for *you,* an alarm that the tired old formulas are failing, that there is a new and better way to set yourself apart and fuel your success.

WAKE-UP CALL #I – SKILLS GUARANTEE NOTHING!

James lives, eats and breathes jobs. He has been running the global recruitment group REED for well over a decade, with offices across Europe, Australasia and the Middle and Far East. REED places hundreds of thousands of people into work every year. His online job site, reed.co.uk, is the biggest in Europe and receives more than 20 million applications per year. When you see tens of millions of people vie for jobs in an intensely competitive and global market, you learn something about what works and what fails.

And one thing we know for sure is that getting the right job comes down to having the right skills. Doesn't it?

When the job market imploded and unemployment surged in the depths of the financial crisis, James attended a special summit on "The Future of Skills". This was an important meeting, since governments and leaders worldwide operate on the same basic assumption or formula: better skills equal better jobs. They invest billions in upgrading people's skills, expecting lower unemployment as a result. Improve your skills and you are more employable, right? Actually, maybe not.

Skills become obsolete, even worthless, more quickly now than ever before. As one of the lead speakers, Lucy Adams, explained, "The trouble is, we don't know which skills will be most in demand in ten years' time."

That's when it dawned on James. "No," he thought. "I cannot possibly know which skills will be most in demand in ten years. Skill requirements constantly change. I know that. But there are some timeless qualities that you absolutely *can* predict every employer will need. I might not know which skills will be most in demand in ten years, but I do know exactly what sort of people I will want to hire in ten years."

He was thinking of the most effective and successful people in his organization and those working for the employers he deals with every year. He was thinking of the bright, capable, flexible people with a strong work ethic and a determination to get things done who have taken his and his clients' companies forward. Good people, of integrity, who are persistent, passionate, energetic, innovative, optimistic and resilient. In short, James, like the thousands of employers we have surveyed since, was thinking about people with the right *mindset*.

WAKE-UP CALL #2 – IT TAKES MORE THAN GUTS TO SUCCEED

Paul is an expert on resilience. His life's work (and obsession) has been built around a simple truth: you cannot necessarily control what happens. But if you can master how you *respond* to what happens, you can craft your destiny. People with guts – the mindset to take on the tough stuff – tend to get ahead. Paul proved this through his thirty years of mindset-related research as the founder and CEO of PEAK Learning, Inc., and the Global Resilience Institute.

Paul is the originator of the Adversity Quotient theory and method. It is the most widely used method in the world for gauging and strengthening human resilience, how people deal with adversity. Top companies use AQ worldwide.

AQ plays big in the world of work. It drives your performance, productivity, innovation, capacity, energy, optimism and ability to achieve your goals. And there are some landmark studies that prove it.

One thing we know for sure: guts matter. The more effectively you handle adversity, the more effective you will be. Right? Again, maybe not.

Paul's wake-up call came from the US prison system. Administrators were asking for AQ training, not for their beleaguered staff but for their prisoners. Paul envisioned the outcome of such training and realized an essential element was missing. Can you imagine creating more resilient, tenacious, determined criminals? Do you really think that's what they need to become successful members of society? That's when Paul, like James, had to confront a brutal truth. It takes more than just guts and resilience to succeed. Paul knew he couldn't take the job until he had a better solution.

––––––––

That's when we (James and Paul) put our heads together to create a master model for the ideal winning mindset – one that goes beyond skills and resilience.

Sometimes the simplest ideas lead to the biggest breakthroughs. We did what we thought was pretty obvious. We asked thousands of top employers what they *really* want in the people they hire, keep, promote and praise. But their answers – and the results of our research testing those answers – may shock you. Our research-based discoveries shatter much of the conventional wisdom and advice on what it takes to get and keep the best jobs, let alone flourish long term in all that you do.

You will discover that much of what we, and perhaps you, assumed would lead to real job success was at least partially off kilter, if not completely wrong.

It all comes down to having the right mindset.

Skills Matter

Let's be clear. Skills matter. They can matter a lot. Your skill set is made up of the tools you employ to live and navigate life. Many jobs require specific skills, and successful employers effectively assess and test for those skills in every job applicant. Before you let a pilot board a plane, you want that pilot to score extremely well on the flight simulator. Skill mastery should be proved, not promised. And if you're seeking work, be prepared to prove what you can do.

Skills count. In fact, your skill set may be why you were hired and may have elevated you to where you are today. In some jobs, especially highly specialized jobs such as actuarial accounting, ultrasound engineering and Arabic-language translating, possessing a specific skill set is absolutely essential.

But relying entirely on skill set can completely backfire in some serious ways, especially when you consider those you are up against every time you try to improve your prospects at work. If you apply for an airline pilot job today, you are competing against a vastly expanded pool of highly trained applicants. In the wake of the economic crisis and the resulting lay-offs, there is a massive backlog of experienced pilots thrilled to work for half their previous pay. It takes the right mindset, not just any mindset, to prevail against those odds.

Your mindset sets you apart. It equips you to thrive where others fail. Those with a superior mindset navigate the world with uncommon integrity, resilience, goodwill, tenacity, agility, openness and perspective. And these traits matter more and more with each passing year, as the harsh realities of competing in a truly global job market reach even the most remote corners of our population and our planet, and as skill sets need to adjust at an ever faster pace.

One of the reasons more and more American and European MBA programmes send their students to India and China as a required part of their programme is to jar them loose from any complacency. Once they confront the vibrant intensity of the entrepreneurial, determined, possibility-fuelled young people they meet in these (and other) countries, they suddenly realize what they are up against every time they go after a new opportunity.

So What is Mindset?

If your skill set is about what you can do, then your mindset is about what you see, think and believe. You'll soon discover that, for starters, it is not about putting on a bright, shiny display of positive attitude. Mindset is deeper. It is what's within and underneath everything else.

The much-quoted *Oxford English Dictionary* defines "mindset" as "a habitual way of thinking". That's why we think of mindset as much deeper and more profound than anything that is just on the surface. For us it is *the internal lens through which you see and navigate life*. Mindset influences everything you see as well as everything you do.

Let's use nature to help explain this definition of "mindset". If you have ever seen a clear frozen lake, it is like a giant lens to the life below. You can look through the ice and see the fish and life on the other side. As you do, you also see all the debris that was captured in the freezing process. Sometimes it's beautiful, like a fallen leaf caught in a suspended state. Other times it's ugly, like chunks of rotten litter that ruin the view. The point is, whatever is captured in that lens is there until the spring thaw.

Your lens also has a tint, a hue. Imagine if, to you, the entire world were the same colour as the lens on your eye, in the way that tinting the ice would change the colour of the water you see below. If you have blue eyes, the world would seem blue. If the world looks green, then you must have green eyes, and so on. You wouldn't realize your eyes are playing this trick on your brain. To you, if your eyes are blue, the world *is* blue. Full stop. You might even argue with someone who sees green or brown. Clearly that person must be mistaken.

This is the way mindset works. Inside your brain, you combine your personal experiences, natural traits and education to form your unique lens. When you are young, each new experience and lesson can add to the mix, so your mindset remains fairly fluid and dynamic. But as the necessary tweaks to your mindset become increasingly minor and infrequent, your lens begins to solidify. In contrast to moods, which can fluctuate, sometimes radically and instantly, mindset becomes, well, set. *At least until now.*

That's why your mindset, your inner lens, like the ice on the lake, colours everything. It becomes *the* way you see and navigate life. Ultimately, it affects what beauty (or litter) you both see and contribute. But the global nature of the context and the times has induced radical change. This gives mindset a fresh urgency. It grants you more powerful opportunities as you master and apply the principles and tools throughout the remainder of this book.

What Employers Really Want

We asked thousands of top employers, including many of the world's best, about what they really look for in their employees. Their answers will have profound implications for your entire career.

Given the choice between someone with the desired mindset who lacks the complete skill set for the job, and someone with the complete skill set who lacks the desired mindset, a total of 96 per cent of the employers surveyed picked *mindset* over skill set as the key element in those they seek and retain. When asked which is more likely, a person with the right skill set developing the desired mindset, or a person with the desired mindset developing the right skill set, 98 per cent of employers confirmed the latter. And 97 per cent of employers felt more confident predicting the mindset of the people they'll be hiring in five to ten years rather than the required skill set.

We were astonished by the strength of these results. They totally undermine one of the central pillars of the job world: that better skills equal better jobs. Instead, they flip the whole career advice model on its head. The new truth: focus on mindset, and the rest (skill set) will take care of itself.

Mindset utterly trumps skill set. Not by a little, *but by a landslide.* Yet when we ask employers how they currently assess mindset in the people they hire, they tend either to pause pregnantly, laugh nervously or mumble an answer that isn't a real answer. In reality, they come up blank. And when we ask them how important it would be to them to have job candidates and employees who can demonstrate, even *prove* their mindsets, that's when we repeatedly hear employers exclaim, "That'd be *fantastic,*" "That's always been the missing piece" or, one of the most common, "Mindset is *everything.*"

Mindset. Employers know they desperately need it but don't know how to assess or discern it in the people they interview. This is your opportunity to show them what they want.

We asked employers, *"What if your job candidates had some way to prove their mindset? What would you think of that?"* Industry by industry, leader by leader, their answer is the same. In the words of Steve Collins, senior sales director for Mars, Inc., "It would be game-changing."

Harry Hoopis is managing partner of Hoopis Financial Group, a $5 billion financial services agency in Chicago, and is considered by many to be the godfather of the industry, one that hires several million people per year worldwide. Over the past few decades he pioneered many of the innovations that have led to the industry's global expansion and enhanced sophistication.

When asked, *"What if your job candidates had some way to prove their mindset? What would you think of that?"*, Hoopis sat up straight, his eyes intense, and said:

I would hire those people [with the right mindset] in a flash! I mean, let's be honest here. CVs tell you almost nothing, and interviews are, let's face it, basically pure gut. There's no science there. Sure, we use a lot of assessments, but we still miss the mark. They make claims, but don't really gauge mindset. If a job candidate can prove to me that he or she has the right mindset, I want them on board. No question. Then, together, we can figure out the rest. Those are the people who make it happen. Those are the ones we want. Nothing compares to mindset.

His words echo what we hear from most employers. So what does this mean for you?

Nothing compares to mindset. But not just *any* mindset. It turns out there is a specific mindset—based on substantive research—which we call the *3G Mindset,* that both predicts and drives your success. In fact, it predicts and drives a *lot* of factors, including how much money you make.

The Path Forward

The promise we made to you is simple: to multiply your chances of getting the job you want and enjoying uncommon success at work while enriching your life immensely along the way.

To help you grasp the true potential of what you are about to learn, ask yourself these two questions:

1. Beyond mindset, what single thing could I master that could have a greater impact on my overall happiness and success, at work and beyond?
2. Specifically how will I benefit as I understand, gauge and strengthen my mindset in the most effective ways?

The remainder of this book will guide you forward and up along a specific and compelling path to fortify every single stage and opportunity in your working life. Your mindset path has four main stages: understand, gauge, strengthen and apply.

Chapters 1 and 2	**Understand** and discover what we mean by the ideal winning mindset.
Chapter 3	**Gauge** your mindset with the most advanced instrument of its kind, the *3G Panorama*.
Chapters 4 to 7	**Strengthen** your mindset.
Chapters 8 and 9	**Apply** the best of your mindset to get, then advance and flourish in, the best jobs.

We wrote this book to give you a distinct and powerful advantage in your pursuits. We have proof that it will. But the best proof will be your success in putting what follows to real use. Put your mindset to work, and a world of possibilities awaits . . . starting *now*.

THE NEW REALITY: WHAT EMPLOYERS REALLY WANT

> My greatest challenge has been to change the mindset of
> people. Mindsets play strange tricks on us. We see things
> the way our minds have instructed our eyes to see.
> – *Muhammad Yunus, Nobel Prize winner and founder of*
> *the microlending movement to eliminate poverty*

Mindset influences everything you see and everything you do. It is best exercised and offers many of its greatest benefits when you have a clear sense of context. Think of it this way: having an awareness of the surrounding waters and predatory creatures gives a fish a far greater chance of not just surviving, but thriving. And for you the "waters" and the "creatures" have changed dramatically. You may have only a sense of it, but the reality is that you have moved from a little pool into a great big one. This affects the importance and nature of the role your mindset may play.

Gen G—Generation Global

Welcome to Generation Global, a generation more defined by *the* age than your age. Gen G radically redefines both your opportunity—your job market—and your competition. No matter what your age, education or place of residence, you are a member of this, the largest and arguably most important generation in the history of humankind. Read that last line twice. No one before you, before now, has been able to make that claim. *You* can. That's potentially good news for some, bad news for others. And, as you will learn, your mindset will make the difference.

Gone are the old straitjackets based on birth year (baby boomers, Gen X, Gen Y, etc.) when we were expected, usually incorrectly, to think and act in a certain way. Work has been fundamentally transformed, and with it old expectations about how you are supposed to think and behave can be tossed aside. As a member of Gen G you can set the rules.

Khosro Khaloghli was born and raised by a southern Russian father from Azerbaijan and a Turkish mother in a dirt-poor neighbourhood in Iran. His mother would stuff old newspapers into his worn-out shoes to help his torn-up feet stay warm on the long walks to and from school in the brutal winter cold.

Through years of hard work, he scraped together $600 to go to the United States on a wrestling scholarship, where he arrived with almost no money, no connections and no knowledge of the English language. Beginning with his first job as the youngest "roughneck" working on the oil rigs in the Persian Gulf, and working his way up in every entry-level job he ever took on, he has shattered all assumptions about what can or cannot be done, and worked (and run companies and/or projects) all over the world.

According to Khosro, "Mindset is *everything!*" (a common quote from our interviews). His entire life has been about putting his mindset to work to make something out of nothing, to grow opportunities when none existed and to prove constantly that the impossible is possible. We could write volumes about Khosro and his amazing story (and someone should), but this book is about *your* story, not Khosro's. So let's fast-forward through the countless jobs he took on, and how he found a way to distinguish himself in each one, using many of the same principles taught in this book.

Today he runs several companies; has achieved a doctorate in urban economics; is participating in the biggest development project in the world in China; lives in the United States and Japan; has achieved immense wealth, which he uses to deliver good to those in need in dozens of countries every day; and continues to work at full pace globally.

At seventy-one, "Dr K" is fitter (no exaggeration) than anyone you know or, most likely, have ever met, has more energy and drive than the most impressive young recruit and learns with the hunger of a new student. Dr K emphatically waves off any attempt to label or group him with a certain generation, and with his characteristic intensity explains:

> Forget these silly labels. Age means nothing! Where you live means nothing! What advantages or disadvantages you may have mean nothing! You, me, everyone, we are people of the world. Everything we do, every job we have, is part of the world. In every job you go for, the work you do, you compete against everyone, everywhere, all the time. That is the reality. That is the opportunity! And that is why I am convinced, please listen to me, that this is the most exciting time in history!

Dr K is right. Your path need not be determined by when and where you were born or the cards you were dealt.

➡ Generation Global, or Gen G, is a generation defined more by *the* age than by *their* age. Gen G includes the 2.5 billion people worldwide who seek any form of rewarding work in an intensely global marketplace.

Forget about your age and instead consider your *stage*. This is what will affect how you can best put your mindset to work. As you read through the Gen G stages, try to determine which stage best defines where you are now. Like Dr K, you may find that you fit into more than one. You will then apply all the tools and tips in this book to your particular reality and challenges.

Up-and-Comers are those who are largely unfazed by the realities, challenges and opportunities the global economy offers. In fact, if you are an up-and-comer, you will embrace them simply because you know no other world. You simply aspire to play your part, make your contribution and land the right kind of work, which allows you to live your relatively uncompromising values, even if it starts with just making a living.

The up-and-comers have a head start over the rest when it comes to specific facets of skill set and mindset, but not enough of one to guarantee success. Likewise, there are specific aspects of mindset that may challenge up-and-comers. Being focused, for example, is an essential component of a winning mindset. Yet the up-and-comers grew up as the most ADD-as-normal age group in human history. And as you will learn later in this book, the more connected you are, the more shallow and unfocused your thought process may become without the right mindset.

Builders are in the throes of work. If you are a builder, you have embarked on some sort of career or work path in which you are prepared to invest considerable energy. You aspire to make life better for yourself and your family and you aspire to make your future prospects even brighter. As a builder, you may be between or considering making changes to the job(s) that make up your grander work path, driven by the desire that your next career move be even more meaningful and rewarding.

Chances are, you, like most builders, learned how to play the game, perhaps through difficult circumstances. You may have achieved what you have so far by taking care of "number one", being politically astute and doing what it takes to win, even if, unfortunately, others have to lose. Your motto may be 'Watch my back, develop a thick skin and be visible to those who might influence my future.'

You've got to be tough. Right? Someone might have once told you, "Nice guys finish last." That's a lie, and we'll prove it. In fact, "nice guys" can have a special edge to finish first. But nice isn't enough. You need to be nice *and* tough.

Let's be fair. Yes, tenacity, guts, mental toughness and being tuned into the world around you are vital aspects of mindset. However, trust, goodwill, compassion and authenticity, as examples, happen to matter as much or more. We will show you why and how.

Likewise, many builders have progressed to a certain point by relying mostly on the merits of skill set, paying only passing respect to mindset. This is a dangerously limiting perspective. If that describes you, a shift in emphasis is now required.

The importance of mindset must become ingrained inside of you. Since you began your working life, the winds of global change have intensified, expanded and thus permeated reality considerably. For some, the winds represent a forbidding chill. For others, they are a balmy, exotic force, filling their sails for future adventures. Your mindset will determine the difference.

Finishers are those aspiring to complete their work-rich years on a positive, fulfilling note. You may dread the thought of having your life, your contribution and yourself shrunk by external forces and seismic shifts.

The mindset aspects of "agility" and its companion, "grit", now come to the fore. We will use these terms a lot throughout this book. If these qualities did not exist before, they must be mustered now.

Finishers perceive the new global playing field as everything from threat to promise. Some embrace it, and others begrudgingly accept it as the new holographic context within which they must wholeheartedly engage in order to finish their careers strongly.

Where do you stand? Are you an up-and-comer, a builder or a finisher? Defining your stage will help you start to understand what you need to do to tap the boundless potential of Generation Global fully. And we cannot emphasize enough the importance of embracing Gen G in developing a winning mindset.

We will refer to Gen G and the three life stages throughout this book. We will provide you with some groundbreaking new tools that will be essential for you to get the most from Gen G, no matter what your stage in life.

What Employers Really Want

As we found in the introduction, employers almost uniformly claim they would hire, promote and retain, as well as bet on, the right *mindset* over the right skill set.

But exactly why are employers so adamant about mindset, and how does it play as you move up the organization? In our research we received scores of comments expressing the intense importance of mindset. As a sampler, consider these five employers' perspectives.

THE REAL STORY – EMPLOYERS' PERSPECTIVES

When asked if mindset was more or less important for leaders, April Pack, senior sales capability and performance manager at Mars, Inc., said, *"At that level, mindset is the most important. We assume they have the skill set. But for anyone who wants to lead anyone, mindset is the most important thing."*

———

Barry Hoffman is HR director of Computacenter, the largest independent provider of IT infrastructure services in Europe, with revenues of £2.5 billion. It is a fast-moving entrepreneurial business where high-level technical skills are essential. Yet to him, skills aren't the differentiator. *"We need mindset,"* he said. *"Skills can be trained and our industry is fast-moving, so a skill today may only have eighteen months' currency because the technology moves so quickly. What we want is the mindset more than skills that may well be out of date in a short time."*

———

Education is a very different kind of business, but as one of Britain's youngest head teachers when she was first appointed principal and CEO of the West London Academy, Hilary Macaulay has had to deliver from day one. *"I think that the bottom line from my experience is that a skill set can be developed and coached and learned in a lot of cases,"* she explained. *"But if you don't have people with the right mindset buying into what's important, then energies can be channelled in completely the wrong way. Finding people with the right mindset is what matters most to me when I add people to my team."*

———

Caitlin Dooley is a contract recruiter for Facebook, one of the hottest companies in the world, with a market value of $37 billion and half a billion users. When asked how important mindset is to their pioneering company, Caitlin responded, *"Skills are easy to find. In fact, they are assumed. We have to look beyond mere technical capabilities. Every two to three months we do the Hackathon! These are all-night coding events, across teams. Many of our most popular products were conceived and built out at a Hackathon. People who thrive on Hackathons and at Facebook absolutely have to have the right mindset, period. That's what's driving us into the future."*

———

Paul Milliken is a vice president of human resources at Shell, advising on recruitment decisions within a global corporation that employs more than a hundred thousand people in more than ninety countries and territories. He explained that one day a manager had come to him with a real dilemma. This manager simply couldn't decide between a highly skilled candidate and another with lower-level skills but the desired mindset.

Milliken said to the manager, *"Look back over your career and think about the successes and failures you have had."* There was silence as the manager thought through recruitment decisions he had made in the past and what the consequences of each had been. Then the truth hit home, and he knew what decision to make. Whenever he had chosen mindset over skills, he realized, *"It works out right."*

Other global leaders are upfront about their recruitment policy. "We are aggressively inclusive in our hiring," Google's website proclaims. "As we continue to grow we are always looking for those who share a commitment to creating search perfection and having a great time doing it." For Google, it's clearly about mindset, as it is for many of the world's most advanced companies.

We have spoken directly to these and other leading employers across Europe, Asia and the Americas, including Aviva, Merck, Prudential, DIRECTV, General Mills, Ernst & Young and Deloitte. All of them fervently agree that mindset trumps skill set not just when they choose whom to employ but when assessing how much value a given person actually delivers and how likely they are to keep that person, long term.

We asked these employers a simple question: "So, specifically how much is someone with the right mindset worth to you, compared to an ordinary hire?" When the answer was vague, like "A lot!", we asked them to quantify their answers. The result is astounding. On average, these top global employers told us that a person with the right mindset is *seven times* more valuable.

> ➡ Put another way, they frankly, even adamantly, admitted that they would gladly trade roughly seven "normal" co-workers for the one rare person with the right mindset.

When we asked hundreds of employers, "If you were forced to make dramatic cuts in your workforce today, whom would you keep, no matter what?" *A hundred per cent state that the person they would keep, no matter what, would have to be the person with the right mindset.*

Skill set matters, but mindset prevails. And skill set is often assumed. Mindset sets you apart. Consider the vital mindset–skill set link.

The Mindset–Skill Set Link

If you are fully skilled, that's great, even though top employers are decisively saying that exceptional skill doesn't necessarily make *you* great. With the right mindset you can go even further. And if you are under-skilled, don't panic. If your skills aren't up to scratch, or if your education and skills training is slightly out of date, the right mindset can help you close the gap.

What our research and these employers are telling you is that if you learn to gauge and grow the right mindset, you will more naturally and easily find and gain the right skill set to secure the future you want. Mindset fuels skill set. These top employers are telling you that mindset comes *first*. Only with the right mindset will you grow and optimize your skill set in the way that works out best.

There's a second strong message the world's top employers would like you to hear. It has to do with the *ingredients* of mindset.

The Key Qualities of the Winning Mindset

Our research team directly asked more than eight hundred employers across all industries what they meant by mindset. More specifically, which mindset qualities or elements do they value most in the people they hire and retain? Based on our prior research, we gave them an exhaustive menu from which to choose, as well as the option to add anything we might have omitted. We forced them to rate each element as essential, desirable or not important.

Before we reveal the results, take a moment to do this micro-challenge. Throughout the book, we'll present you with a series of these microchallenges to help you apply and internalize the key lessons.

Microchallenge:
What Employers Really Want

Ask yourself these three questions. Feel free to write your answers in the spaces provided.

1

If you were an employer, what specific mindset qualities would you want most in the people you hire?

A. _____

_____

_____

_____

2

What mindset qualities does a person need in order to have the greatest chance of promotion or moving ahead in his or her career?

A. _____

_____

_____

_____

3

Think about the people closest to you in life. What specific aspects of them or their mindset do you most admire? Which ones attract you? If you could have a group of friends who possessed any elements of mindset, which elements would you choose?

A. _____

_____

_____

_____

_____

Now look at your full list. How much do your answers to each of these questions vary? Or, like our thousands of employers, do you find yourself coming up with essentially the same list?

Let's see if the world's employers and you agree. Check out the "Top Twenty Mindset Qualities" list from our multi-year global research effort. This list is exceptionally robust. For all twenty of these mindset qualities, more than 90 per cent of employers listed them as "essential" or "desirable".

What struck us was not which ones people chose. Rather, we were amazed by how consistent the lists were across industries, countries and cultures. Mindset is both universal and timeless. This means – unlike skill set – that if you master it, you can take it anywhere and use it for ever.

Employers' Top Twenty Mindset Qualities		
Rank	**Quality**	**Essential/Desirable**
1	honesty	100%
1	trustworthiness	100%
3	commitment*	99.77%
4	adaptability	99.77%
5	accountability**	98.6%
6	flexibility	98.6%
7	determination	98.14%
8	loyalty	97.91%
9	relationship building	97.44%
10	contribution	97.44%
11	sincerity	96.98%
12	balance	96.28%
13	fairness	96.05%
14	morality	96.05%
15	drive	95.81%
16	collaborative focus	95.35%
17	energy	95.12%
18	purposefulness	93.49%
19	openness	93.49%
20	innovativeness	93.02%

* Commitment: We have rated this above adaptability because 92.09% of employers told us that commitment was an essential quality. Adaptability was rated as essential by only 75.12% of employers.

** Accountability has been rated above flexibility because 72.56% of employers told us that accountability was an essential quality, whereas only 66.51% rated flexibility as essential.

Take a moment not just to read through, but to *ponder* the list slowly. How do you think you stack up? How would you honestly rate yourself against the people who are the absolute strongest at these qualities? How does your list compare to this list? You may be using different words, but our guess is that many of yours match these.

It's important for you to know that the top twenty is by no means the entire list. There are many more elements of mindset that employers seek and our research substantiates as among the most important. These additional traits will round out the winning mindset you will grow throughout this book. This is merely the top of the list. In the next chapter, we'll present this list in a different way to help you see how it forms part of the vital foundation of mindset.

And, of course, saying or listing these qualities is a lot different from breaking them down in a way they can be put to real use or truly gauged and strengthened. So the list is long, but it's worth noting what ended up at the very top.

THE TOP SIX MINDSET QUALITIES

Take a look at the traits employers tended to put at the very top of their lists. Honesty and trustworthiness tie for first place, with 100 per cent of top employers marking them as essential or desirable. Not a single employer said that these qualities were not important, and more than 90 per cent said that they were essential. Commitment, adaptability, accountability and flexibility all follow closely behind. This means that if you truly mastered just these six, as a starting point, your value to employers grows dramatically.

Starting with the top six, and eventually expanding to the entire list presented later in the book, you'll ultimately want to demonstrate these specific mindset qualities in all you do, especially in the toughest moments, not just when it's convenient.

MINDSET MATTERS

Throughout the remainder of the book, we will show you how to strengthen the top traits within yourself. Understanding mindset is critical. And you've got a strong start. The real power comes when you understand, gauge, strengthen and apply the right mindset in all you do.

But don't take our word for it. Listen to what some employers say:

"What's the point in having an individual with the complete skills if they haven't got the right mindset in which to use them? Someone with the right mindset will be more than willing to learn and develop the skills required, giving you the perfect candidate!" – Melissa Mezzone, Geopost UK

"Mindset is everything. Period. Skill set is assumed. I have had more than 100,000 people working for me, and I expect people to be competent at their jobs. If they aren't they don't belong there. But getting people who have the right mindset—that rare combination of authenticity and integrity, determination and resilience, as well as being connected to and taking into account the big picture—that's the only way we can win." – John Suranyi, former president, DIRECTV

"Mindset is so important. I had a very skilled employee here last year who came very well recommended and had a great list of skills. But despite being very impressive at interview, she just didn't want to work, had no enthusiasm, curiosity, entrepreneurship—big mistake that I was fooled in the interview into thinking that the skills were so important." – Ben Glazier, Glazier Publicity

Shattering Old Assumptions

For years we have been taught, "Get a good education. Get some experience." The emphasis has typically been on developing our individual expertise and knowledge as the sure path to success. And, as we said, these standard CV builders matter, but they fall short.

This means that, chances are, like most people, your CV, job searches, interviews, training and other career-related efforts will have, until now, all emphasized education, experience, training, capabilities—things related to skill set—first and foremost. Don't feel bad. That's normal. In fact, it's what virtually all the job experts tell you to do.

More than 2 million people apply for jobs through James's firm, REED, every month. A huge number of their CVs follow the same skill set-based formula. Through their CVs each applicant is saying, "Here's what I've done, here's what I learned, and here's what I know how to do." This standard formula all too often completely misses the mark on mindset. We think this offers you a powerful opportunity.

Later in the book we'll teach you some simple tips to literally triple your chances of winning the job you want, even over other, more qualified candidates. But first you need a firm foundation on what the winning mindset is all about.

Imagine buying a house. You want a home that will really last, so what you truly care about is the structural integrity, the quality of construction, as well as how well it's wired, plumbed and designed. You know these items will determine the long-term value. But every time you speak to an estate agent, he talks to you about the landscaping, finishes and the ownership history of the house. These aspects might make the house *appear* attractive, but they do little to answer your real questions. They don't address what you really want. Without even knowing it, this is exactly what happens when applicants provide and employers receive the standard CVs. In this sense, when it comes to winning today's game with yesterday's rules, all bets are off.

CHAPTER RECAP

Generation Global (Gen G)
is the largest generation in human history.

Up-and-Comers
are entering or are already engaged in the early years of their careers.

Builders
are in the middle of their careers, with many years behind and ahead.

Finishers
are in the closing years of their careers, seeking their final legacy, before it's over.

Employers desperately want mindset over skill set. Mindset trumps and grows skill set.

The skill set–mindset link: if you learn to gauge and grow the right mindset, you will more naturally and easily find and gain the right skill set to secure the future you want.

Mindset, in general, is not enough. There is a winning or ideal mindset.

Employers' Top Six Mindset Qualities
include: honesty, trustworthiness, commitment, adaptability, accountability and flexibility.

There is a superior formula for developing the winning mindset. And it's one you can begin to master now.

THE WINNING MINDSET: INTRODUCING 3G

The empires of the future are empires of the mind.
— *Winston Churchill*

Not all mindsets are created equal. Imagine taking all the top mindset ingredients top employers say make the biggest difference, pressure-testing them to see how they hold up and then pouring them into a giant sorting machine. That's essentially what we've done to arrive at what we call the "3G Mindset".

The 3G Mindset is a distillation of all the most important mindset qualities which employers seek, and science substantiates, into three fundamental categories. These three categories provide a logical, accessible and memorable framework that includes all the key mindset ingredients.

We've found that all the most important aspects of your mindset fit into these three categories, or three "Gs", which stand for Global Mindset, Good Mindset and Grit Mindset. You will discover how each term or "G" is drawn from the scientific research and vetted in the practical world of business. Taken together, these aspects create the 3G Mindset. You will learn how to master—to gauge, strengthen and apply—these aspects in powerful ways in the upcoming chapters.

The 3G Mindset encompasses and goes beyond the top six and top twenty mindset qualities. The 3G model is based on the entire list, both of what employers really want and what the best science says makes the biggest difference. The elements of the 3G Mindset come from our worldwide research, including an in-depth look at those people most of us would admire, even aspire to be more like.

No matter where you are in life—whether you are an up-and-comer, builder or finisher—the 3Gs apply to you. However, depending on your stage within Gen G, you simply may apply the 3Gs differently.

We discovered that another revolutionary feature of the 3G Mindset is that, unlike skill set, these three Gs are equally powerful for a CEO, an entrepreneur, a middle manager, a retail clerk, a dockworker or a part-time administrator. We believe, and have proved, that these same ingredients can therefore be applied for anyone, anywhere. You can use the 3G Mindset to improve your prospects, not just at work but through-out your life.

"As one of the biggest insurance companies in the world, we are literally shaping our entire pan-European culture of 10,000 employees and 18,500 salespeople around a clear set of values and behaviours. We are building a new mindset to win in an intensely competitive marketplace. I did not know what to call it. But now I do. We will use these 3G-based principles to guide how we hire, retain and develop our people. I firmly believe a 3G workforce will both delight our customers and stake holders, as well as prove to be our fiercest competitive weapon." – Andrea Moneta, chief executive officer Europe, Aviva plc

The 3Gs—global, good and grit—explain the profound difference between bottom and top performers, poor and wealthy entrepreneurs, stagnating and promoted employees, being fully engaged versus being permanently enraged, those who are valued and retained versus those who are happily let go, those who earn the most and those who earn the least, as well as those who are hired versus those who are fired.

The 3G Mindset answers for you this vital question:

> ➥ Of all the aspects of mindset, what are the three most powerful and important aspects for me to focus on to grow the career and life I want?

For example, we have discovered that the 3G Mindset predicts how much money you tend to make. There's a significant relationship between these two factors. And while money may not be your top priority, it probably matters to you at some level. We will share and explore these findings and more in the following chapters.

Through our research, we tested the elements that make up the 3G Mindset as well as their overall construct against the insights of top thinkers, leaders and research worldwide, as well as frontline employers. The 3Gs hit the mark.

Whether you aspire to lead or follow, that's what the rest of this book will provide—the tools and insights you will need to master the right mindset, the 3G Mindset, to get and keep the job you want.

Global comes first, as it is the *vantage point* of the 3G mindset. It is about how far you see, reach and go to understand and address the everyday challenges and issues. Global has surged in importance, and it's here to stay.

According to Dr Steve Cohen, "a global mindset has emerged as the defining factor in a person's long-term career prospects and growth. What most people don't realize is a global mindset is now essential for everyone, in every job, in every industry. It's no longer for the exclusive club of global business leaders. You cannot fulfil your career potential without a global mindset."

In a 2003 study by Marshall Goldsmith, he and his team interviewed a diverse group of human resources executives in two hundred global organizations. They were asked to name the most important leadership skills (with 1 = unimportant and 10 = extremely important, from a list of 72 items) required for effectiveness in the past, present and future.

Not surprisingly, the top three items mentioned for past leaders did not include any that remotely suggested global considerations. But when asked what will be important for the future, the third most highly rated item was "makes decisions that reflect global considerations". Today this item ranks among the top of many recruiters' criteria for the people they hire for most positions.

As a member of Gen G, you cannot succeed without mastering this Global Mindset. The 3G Mindset is designed to set you apart and allows you to compete for jobs at any level on a global scale. Arguably, the global facet of mindset is what sets humans apart. It drives us to be uniquely curious and relentlessly inventive. You might say it is essential to our evolution. And you may be pleased to learn that global is not age dependent. People at any stage and age can master global.

Global is about openness to new experiences and new ideas as well as the ability to make new connections and to create new combinations. Global means—regardless of age, job level or position—that you must demonstrate unprecedented cultural agility and alacrity in order to remain viable and marketable, starting *now*.

The world is not only intensely interconnected, it is increasingly boundaryless and boundless. Yet global is not only or even centrally about working with people across country boundaries. Instead global reveals that those who limit their *vantage point* limit their possibilities. Those who elevate their perspective, who learn to consider and tap an ever-expanding world of influences and resources, are those who embrace the global mindset.

"We run the biggest call centre business in the world. We operate in twenty-six countries. As a leader, I've come to realize that everyone—even, and perhaps *especially* the person working in the entry level job on the front line—has to have a global mindset. To have a future in our company, our 65,000 people at all levels have to operate with an appreciation for the world well beyond their village or cubicle. That's the world of business today." – Chad Carlson, chief operations officer, the Americas, Sitel

A global perspective can change a person from being locked into a closed, destructive mindset to allowing them to take a new and productive path forward.

Good comes next, because good is the *bedrock* upon which everything else is built. This facet of mindset is about seeing and approaching the world in a way that truly benefits those around you. It encompasses ethics, morality and your general approach to others. While global may define the context of your contribution, and grit may determine its magnitude, good determines how positive (or negative) your contribution to your job, your life and the world ends up being.

Good, like the entire 3G Mindset, has a powerful ripple and contagious effect, at all job levels. If you are or ever aspire to be a leader in any sense, it's especially important to grow as much good as possible. In a landmark study, Michael Brown, Linda Trevino and David Harrison, professors in organizational behaviour and political science, proved that the qualities that make up a Good Mindset affect how honest, considerate, trusting, fair, dedicated and satisfied one's followers would be. The degree of good also determines how you as a leader are rated and valued by others. In short, you cannot lead others effectively without a Good Mindset.

Good is timeless. And its importance in how much you give and how you are perceived at work has long been established. Thirty-two years ago Kathryn Bartol at the University of Maryland established that the degree to which many of these Good Mindset qualities exist has a significant impact on your commitment level and likelihood to quit. This is a strong message to leaders and followers alike: a Good Mindset is good for business. It also leads to stronger engagement and commitment in whatever job you choose.

Given the dog-eat-dog competitiveness of most businesses today, it may have surprised you to learn that the timeless virtues—honesty and trustworthiness—are the chart-toppers in the eyes of the best employers. Where can any enterprise go, and how long can it flourish without these elements?

The reason employers want you to excel in these, along with all the components of good, is because they make you and them shine. Good is absolutely *fundamental* and instrumental to the long-term successful operation of any organization or social group. What the world's employers are telling you is that good guys *don't* finish last. And we will prove it to you in the coming chapters.

> "If you don't have integrity, you can see through it straight away. Quite often in business highly ambitious people are just in it for themselves and people begin to say, 'Is he a team player?' and you lose a bit of trust. Even if you've got a lot of drive, you're on a tricky wicket. Walking the talk is really important. Trust is the biggest thing in business, I think—if you can't trust somebody, how can you do business with them?" – Chris Zanetti, regional VP Europe, Merck Consumer Healthcare

A vivid appreciation of the fundamental importance of good will act as a rock upon which individual decisions and actions will rightfully be made.

Grit is the third G and the *fuel cell* of the 3G Mindset: it propels you forward and brings your 3G Mindset to life, even in the darkest moments. When you consider the top six facets of mindset, *none* of them can be effectively and consistently demonstrated (or sustained) without a significant degree of grit.

Grit proves anyone can come out ahead, regardless of his or her advantages or disadvantages in life. Grit shatters the entitlement myth—the belief that a certain education, certain grades or certain privileges guarantee a good job—that has infected and weakened the United States, the United Kingdom and many of the world's wealthiest countries. It is grit, often combined with the other Gs, that inspires us.

Drawing from a deep well of scientific rigour and in-the-business-trenches proof, we will show you how individuals with grit demonstrate sheer tenacity, resilience and the relentlessness to win, and to win big. Grit can be both scientifically measured and permanently improved. In the following chapters, we'll show you how.

Whenever you watch an Olympic event and you see that one athlete who stumbles, gets edged out or even injured but, rather than give up, digs deep and wins, you are seeing true grit in motion. The same admirable mindset applies brilliantly to every facet of getting and growing your career.

In a rapidly changing, adversity-rich world, grit is the quality that enables us to pick ourselves up, dust ourselves off and carry on, stronger for the experience.

It is important to remember that the winning 3G Mindset is a single, practice-forged lens through which you see and navigate the world; it is not three separate lenses that you put on and take off like fashion eyewear. The 3Gs frequently overlap and fuse with one another, as you can see below, to give your lens its own special quality:

As we've indicated in the updated table on page 34, the top twenty qualities the employers seek in their hires can often be assigned to more than one of the Gs. As the 3Gs blend, they become stronger. It is this natural meld that enriches the entire 3G Mindset model and renders it uniquely powerful.

Look at the results for yourself. Look at the top twenty through the 3G lens. The better you understand what the world's top employers are saying, the better your prospects are sure to be. In fact, you can use this list as evidence of what they want, and what you need to emphasize. Notice how naturally every single item in the top twenty list fits one or more of the 3Gs.

The 3G Mindset—Employers' Top Twenty			
Rank	**Quality**	**3G**	**Essential/Desirable**
1	honesty	good	100%
2	trustworthiness	good	100%
3	commitment	grit	99.77%
4	adaptability	global	99.77%
5	accountability	grit	98.6%
6	flexibility	global	98.6%
7	determination	grit	98.14%
8	loyalty	good	97.91%
9	relationship building	global/good	97.44%
10	contribution	global/good	97.44%
11	sincerity	good	96.98%
12	balance	global/good	96.28%
13	fairness	good	96.05%
14	morality	good	96.05%
15	drive	grit	95.81%
16	collaborative focus	global/good	95.35%
17	energy	grit	95.12%
18	purposefulness	grit	93.49%
19	openness	global/good	93.49%
20	innovativeness	global/grit	93.02%

But before you go too far, look at the data from a different angle. What happens when we pick those items employers are *most* intense about? If we disregard what employers considered merely desirable and re-rank the qualities based on what employers considered most essential, you will see that an interesting thing happens. "Commitment" jumps up to the top of the list.

	The Top Twenty Mindset Qualities Ranked by Essential Qualities, in Descending Order			
Rank	Quality	3G	Essential	Desirable
1 (+2)	commitment	grit	**92.09%**	7.67%
2 (−1)	honesty	good	**91.4%**	8.6%
3 (−2)	trustworthiness	good	**90.93%**	9.07%
4 (−)	adaptability	global	**75.12%**	24.65%
5 (−)	accountability	grit	**72.56%**	26.05%
6 (+2)	loyalty	good	**71.63%**	26.28%
7 (−)	determination	grit	**71.4%**	26.74%
8 (−2)	flexibility	global	**66.51%**	32.09%
9 (−)	contribution	global/good	**66.51%**	30.93%
10 (+5)	drive	grit	**62.09%**	33.72%
11 (+2)	morality	good	**61.4%**	34.65%
12 (+2)	fairness	good	**59.3%**	36.74%
13 (−3)	relationship building	global/good	**59.07%**	38.37%
14 (−3)	sincerity	good	**56.28%**	40.7%
15 (+2)	energy	grit	**53.72%**	41.4%
16 (−)	collaborative focus	global/good	**52.79%**	42.56%
17 (−5)	balance	global/good	**46.98%**	49.3%
18 (−)	openness	global/good	**44.19%**	49.3%
19 (−)	purposefulness	grit	**37.21%**	56.28%
20 (−)	innovativeness	global/grit	**34.65%**	58.37%

There are two key lessons for you from this data. The first is about intensity and the second is about authenticity. Number one, pay keen attention to how intense employers really are about commitment. We discovered that they are really saying that genuine commitment is increasingly rare and exceptionally valuable. This means this single mindset quality offers particular power.

> "Kids feed off staff, and if you are not committed then they are not committed. So for me, committing myself 100 per cent is part of the job." – Charlotte Bowater, teacher, West London Academy

Number two, don't even think about attempting to put your best foot forward for any opportunity without demonstrating an authentic and deep sense of commitment. Like all of the 3G Mindset qualities, commitment cannot be faked. When it is missing, it's almost impossible to shine. But when it's truly there, commitment can help you win when the odds are stacked against you.

Commitment has an exceptionally powerful effect. It stirs the soul, engenders trust, earns respect and kindles our admiration. You no doubt can think of your examples. Here are a few of ours.

THE REAL STORY—COMMITMENT/ HONESTY/TRUSTWORTHINESS

James remembers a true-life example: "Dave was an armed robber. I had heard about Dave from colleagues. He had just been released after twenty years in prison and he had signed up with one of our welfare-to-work programmes. As you can imagine, Dave didn't exactly walk into the first job he applied for. In fact, as time passed he became increasingly frustrated with the job search process. Some of his old associates noticed this and one even offered him 'a job' as a getaway driver that would have paid £10,000 for just one night's work. He was close to accepting this offer when a REED client came up with an alternative: working the night shift in a maintenance gang on the railways."

Dave decided to take the job on the railways. And he approached his new, clean path with tremendous commitment. James went to meet him because he wanted to hear firsthand why he had made certain decisions in his life. Dave's appearance was certainly striking. He was a very big man with a shaved head. And yet he was quietly spoken and thoughtful and came across as a natural leader. "I didn't want to spend my whole life looking over my shoulder," he said. "I wanted to make an honest living without having to worry every time there was a knock on the door."

James asked him how he found working nights. "He looked at me as if I were daft and said, 'I've always worked nights . . . not that the taxman knew about it.'"

Not long after, Dave was promoted to supervisor and later he returned to prison, not as an inmate this time but to talk to young prisoners about why they shouldn't follow the same path that he had.

Dave had changed his mindset and in doing so he had changed his life. Obviously, he originally fell far short of ideal when it came to the honest and trustworthy stakes. But through the commitment he showed to a tough job that required him to work antisocial hours in all weather, he regained his freedom and with it his dignity. "Good" for Dave was a choice, and he demonstrated considerable grit in exercising that choice.

James recalls another job seeker whom his company worked with who showed true grit and true commitment to turn his situation around.

Joseph was from east London. He had been out of work for six years. His confidence had taken a knock and he had become increasingly isolated and depressed. He was referred by the government-run Jobcentre Plus to a mandatory programme run by

REED for people who had become long-term unemployed. Once in the programme, Joseph worked closely with his personal adviser and gradually took some tentative steps towards returning to work.

Slowly his confidence grew. He started attending interviews and eventually he was offered a job working as a security guard. Joseph accepted. Once he started work, the change in him was immediate. It was as obvious as the difference between night and day. So much did he change, in fact, that when REED asked for a volunteer from those who had successfully passed through the programme to speak about their experience to an audience of 800 people at a government-run conference, Joseph stepped forward.

When the allotted day came, and Joseph stood up to speak at the Queen Elizabeth Conference Centre, in the shadow of the British Houses of Parliament, the audience sat in utter silence. There was not so much as a cough or a sniffle as Joseph told his story. He described how he had been to hell and back and that he would not wish his experience on anyone. He told them that he had found it so hard to pick himself up from the floor that he had almost given up trying. And he told them that now that he was back at work he had rediscovered what it was to be a man.

Joseph ended his speech by saying that for the first time in six years he had been able to buy his children Christmas presents. The audience, many of whom were moved to tears, gave him a standing ovation.

Joseph gave this speech many years ago and people still talk about it. Here was a man who had changed his mindset so fundamentally that he had gone from being a person who could barely venture outdoors to doing something that most people say they are most afraid of, speaking to a large audience of strangers. And it was no ordinary speech he gave. It was a magnificent, inspiring speech that our colleagues who help people back into work still refer to. Joseph's journey was a testament to his grit and to his commitment.

We highlight these stories of commitment not just because employers crave it so intensely, but because it is exactly the mindset quality you must demonstrate to get the most out of your efforts to put your mindset to work.

But what of those two other qualities ranked in the employers' top six: adaptability and accountability? It would seem that both these qualities have become even more important with the emergence of and across all three stages of Gen G.

Over our decades of work and research with top companies around the world, we have witnessed firsthand the intensification around these two qualities. When asked, "If you could have your employees be more of anything, what would you want it to be?", those saying "accountable" and/or "adaptable" (to change and uncertainty) have risen from a quiet murmur to a thunderous chorus. These qualities are typically at or near the top.

These are big companies employing millions of people per year combined. We also like to ask the questions the other way around: "What effect would it have on your business if your people were measurably more accountable (or adaptable)?" Answers usually range from exclamations such as "Transformational!" "Huge!" and "Tremendous!" to more analytical thoughts, such as "It would make us much more efficient." "We'd get much more done." And "It's the only way we can compete going forward."

James learned that, for Gen G, adaptability is a given. It was a lesson he learned from one of his young graduate trainees. And it turned out to be a very valuable lesson indeed.

THE REAL STORY—ADAPTABILITY

In the relatively early days of the Internet, just before the millennium, Paul Rapacioli, the young man who was then running the REED website, came into James's office with an idea.

Rapacioli thought that REED should open up its website so that any user, including the company's competitors, could use the site for free. In a clever play on words, he had called his idea "freecruitment". He argued that by allowing others free access to the site, there would be more jobs posted there, which would in turn encourage more people to visit.

James could hardly believe what he was hearing. And he was immediately appalled by the idea. Rapacioli's proposal flew directly in the face of his commercial instincts. James had grown up knowing that winning business in a competitive world was what put food on the table, and he had been completely conditioned to be a fiercely competitive person.

James hated the idea of letting competitors use his precious website. But the more he thought about it, the more he realized that Paul Rapacioli was on to something. The idea was based on a simple and persuasive premise: that "a crowd attracts a crowd". "Freecruitment" offered REED the chance to create the job market online, and the risks involved didn't seem that great. After all, if it didn't work, he could always change his mind. James was persuaded. It was time to think big, to think global.

"Freecruitment" was launched in the spring of 2000. It took off immediately and, with the benefit of hindsight, it is fair to say that Paul Rapacioli's idea was the single most important reason why the REED website grew so rapidly that it became the largest and most successful site for jobs in Europe. It turned out to be a true win-win scenario. It was good for job seekers and good for recruiters.

To this day it is still possible for competitors to post jobs for free on the REED site. And it is now used by more than 80 per cent of the United Kingdom's top recruitment companies. So what happened to Mr Rapacioli? He was paid a bonus of £100,000 for his idea and later moved on to start his own internet business in Sweden.

This situation would never have arisen if it were not for the emergence at the time of transformational new technologies that made such cooperation between competing parties mutually beneficial. Adam Brandenburger, a Harvard Business School professor, invented a new word to describe this phenomenon. He called it "co-opetition". The development of network computing has since brought co-opetition to scores of industries and business services.

Clearly, adaptability is a fundamental aspect of a Global Mindset and a fundamental attribute of Gen G. "Adapt," the saying goes, "or die." Or, as Charles Darwin said, "It is not the fittest that survives but the one that is most adaptable to change." We would change the last part to say, ". . . the one most adaptable to the unexpected."

Now you can consider accountability, the next of the top six, another grit-related quality. What do employers mean when they say that they want people to be accountable? At work we are all accountable to someone. Every organization is accountable to its customers. Individual members of staff are accountable to one another. The chief executive is accountable to the board and the board is accountable to the owners. In the great companies, *everyone* is accountable to the customer.

When you demonstrate accountability at its best, it goes beyond the confines of your job description and becomes a deeper sense of responsibility to *step up* and improve situations over which you have some potential influence. Masters of accountability don't let titles and roles get in the way of making a positive contribution when and where they can.

Accountability is engrained in the fabric of our working lives but, strangely, many people lose sight of it. Maybe this is an easy mistake to make. When things go well, it is tempting to take credit, and when things go badly, it is easy to lay the blame elsewhere. Or perhaps the perceived price for taking accountability and risking a mistake outweighs the potential, but not guaranteed, upside.

In the United States, there is no law that requires you to attempt to resuscitate someone who stops breathing. However, if you do try, you can be sued for any damages resulting from your effort. Sometimes accountability comes with a price. That's why many people step back instead of stepping up when a tough job needs to be done. Why step up if you might get chopped down for doing so? Why not play it safe?

Because often the price for *not* taking accountability is even greater. If someone was dying on the sidewalk next to you and you knew you could help, would you turn away, or would you give it your best? And if the person died, how well would you sleep knowing you could have helped but chose not to? And knowing that the project you are working on or your team's ability to make its plan depends on really stepping up, do you pitch in or let it die? Now that you know accountability is essential to standing out, being noticed and valued, do you step up, or do you let your prospects slowly die?

And remember: "No buck was ever made by passing them."

So far, we have established that when it comes to what employers *really* want, mindset trumps skill set. But not just *any* mindset. Employers are loud and clear:

Mindset matters more: Employers rank mindset above skill set when it comes to decisions on recruitment and promotion.

Mindset fills the gaps: Employers believe that people with the right mindset are far more likely to develop the right skill set than the other way around.

Mindset endures: Employers don't know what sort of skills they will want in ten years, but they are very clear about what sort of mindset they will want.

Mindset secures your job: Employers unanimously chose those people with the right mindset—the 3G Mindset—as the ones they would keep, even when they had to cut everyone else.

Mindset sets you apart: Employers reveal that when you master the 3G Mindset, you are worth more than seven "normal" co-workers.

Mindset and money are married: Our studies reveal that the 3G Mindset, specifically, predicts how much money you make.

Mindset is universal: Employers worldwide are seeking the same mindset at heart. Our global research involving thousands of individuals and organizations shows that the mindset employers really want fits precisely into the three main elements: global, good and grit.

3G applies to you in any job, at any level, in any situation. It applies intensely to the top executives we coach and collaborate with on a broad range of issues. In most cases their success hinges on how well they put 3G to work. When we do 360 feedback exercises to gain insights into top leaders from multiple perspectives, 3G Mindset is what makes the single biggest difference. Nothing else comes close. It determines how well they solve problems, deal with their people, strategize for the future and drive success. It determines how others rate them and whether or not they get to keep or advance within their jobs, from CEO on down.

3G applies with equal force and with equal power to determine your success when you go for your very first job. Even high-powered top executives have to start somewhere. And, in most cases, when we do a careful analysis of their histories, 3G explains what got them to where they are.

These three elements—global, good and grit—are the most important things you need to have and grow to set yourself apart from the rest and to flourish in your career and life. When you begin to master the 3G Mindset, not only can you win the better opportunities that more "qualified" people lose, you will become a better person along the way.

- -

CHAPTER RECAP

There is an ideal winning mindset, called the 3G Mindset.

Global

the vantage point of the 3G Mindset. It is about how far you see, reach, *and* go to understand and address the everyday challenges and issues.

Good

the *bedrock* upon which everything else is built. This facet of mindset is about seeing and approaching the world in a way that truly benefits those around you.

Grit

the *fuel cell* of the 3G Mindset. Having the vantage point (global) and the bedrock (good) is essential, but it is the fuel cell (grit) that propels you forward and brings your 3G Mindset to life, even in the darkest moments.

Employers' Top Twenty and Top Six

Most desired mindset qualities all fall within one of the 3Gs.

- -

You can do all of these, and so much more. Let's start by giving you new insights into your mindset and yourself.

MEASURE YOUR MINDSET: THE 3G PANORAMA

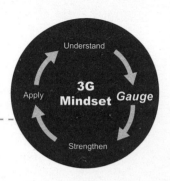

Knowing others is wisdom, knowing yourself
is enlightenment.
— *Lao-Tzu, Chinese Taoist philosopher*

Now that you understand the basics of the 3G Mindset (what it is and why employers crave it), you are ready for the next step, which is to *gauge* or measure your current mindset. To do so, you will complete a powerful new tool, the 3G Panorama, which lays the foundation upon which you can strengthen and apply your 3G Mindset. Or you may opt to complete the briefer, quicker 3G Panorama Preview, provided on the following pages.

Because of its length and detail, the much more robust 3G Panorama is completed online, providing you with a full feedback report. Whether you choose the preview, the full panorama or both, the explanation of 3G throughout this chapter applies to you and your quest to get, keep and flourish in the best jobs.

If you plan to complete the full 3G Panorama, you need not complete the preview—you can flip ahead to the 3G Panorama right now. Otherwise, take a few minutes to complete the following self-assessment:

3G Panorama Preview

Answer each of the following questions. Be completely honest with yourself. Your answers should reflect the current truth about yourself. You want to indicate what *is*, not the way you would *like* to be.

Using a scale of 1 to 10, how would you and the people who see the *real* you (those who know you best) rate you on each of the following dimensions, compared to everyone else, including those who are most exceptional in each of these areas?

Note: 10 is the *highest* possible rating. It means you demonstrate that specific quality *flawlessly* and *consistently*. (Hint: 10s are rare.)

Global

Connected— in touch with and connected to the bigger world.	
Boundaryless—thinking and reaching way beyond your immediate world to get fresh ideas and perspective.	
Open— receptive to a broad range of ideas and perspectives.	
Flexible—readily adapt to change and the unexpected.	
Global—keenly aware of and sensitive to the "ripple effect"—the broader, far-reaching, often invisible impact of your words and deeds.	
Total	

Good

Honest—showing no deceit, telling the full truth, even when it's uncomfortable.	
Moral—consistently focused on doing what's right in any circumstance.	

Dependable—can be counted on to do what you say.	
Caring—showing genuine concern and compassion for others.	
Good—consistently striving to be a good person with and for others.	
Total	

Grit

Growth-oriented—constantly seeking ways to learn, grow and improve.	
Resilient—responding optimally every time adversity strikes.	
Intense—able to consistently remain free from distractions and fully focused on the task at hand.	
Tenacious—refusing to give up, sticking to whatever you decide to pursue.	
Full of grit—Demonstrating uncommon determination and strength in difficult times.	
Total	

SCORING YOUR 3G PREVIEW

Notice there are three sections, with five questions each.

1. Add up the five numbers for each section (Global, Good and Grit) and insert your section total in the blank on the far right column.

2. Add your three Gs or section totals to get your 3G total, and insert it here:

| 3G
Preview
Total |
|---|
| |

Interpreting Your 3G Panorama Preview Results

Remember: The preview is an initial *glimpse* at what your larger 3G Mindset might look like. It provides an initial insight, which most people find tremendously useful. However, given its brevity and simplicity, it's important not to read too much into the numbers. To avoid this problem, we'll speak about scores and ranges in broad, general strokes.

In the preview, the total score possible for each G is 50. Scores for each G fall on a normal distribution similar to the graph below.

INDIVIDUAL G (GLOBAL, GOOD AND GRIT) SCORE DISTRIBUTION

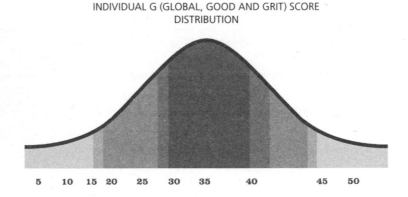

| 5 | 10 | 15 | 20 | 25 | 30 | 35 | 40 | 45 | 50 |

Your total scores can hypothetically range from 15 to 150 points. Overall scores tend to follow the following distribution:

3G TOTAL SCORE DISTRIBUTION PANORAMA PREVIEW

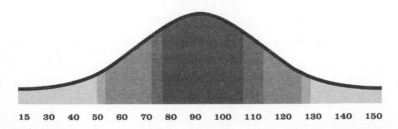

| 15 | 30 | 40 | 50 | 60 | 70 | 80 | 90 | 100 | 110 | 120 | 130 | 140 | 150 |

This gives you a general sense of where you stand overall. The majority of people score in the mid-range of 80 to 110, with fewer people scoring at the high and low extremes.

The higher you score on each of the 3Gs, and on your 3G total, the better. The lower your score, the more you have to work on in order to achieve a truly winning mindset, along with all the advantages it can offer you.

Panorama Microchallenge: Preview

1

On which G did you score the highest? In what way has that G been helpful to you so far?

A.

2

On which G did you score lowest? In what ways, if any, has that G hindered you or held you back from fulfilling your potential?

A.

3 How did you score on your 3G total?

A. _____

_____

4 What does this initially suggest to you about where you are now and how much you may benefit as your 3G Mindset improves?

A. _____

_____

_____

_____

_____

Measuring Your Mindset with the 3G Panorama

To get the full view, access the 3G Panorama. It provides much more detailed and meaningful insights. If you're serious about getting the full picture of where you stand, this is the true gauge.

To access the 3G Panorama, visit www.3GMindset.com/book and follow the instructions on the screen.

The 3G Panorama will help you accurately gauge your 3G Mindset. This assessment is extremely robust. It is grounded in rigorous research, then was built upon and tested through our intensive global studies over the past few years. And the 3G Panorama is predictive. In other words, specific facets of it can actually predict a host of factors, including your performance at work, your health and vitality, how much your boss values you and your contribution and how much money you make.

Our advice is to invest the time, effort and focus to reap the full rewards the 3G Panorama can offer. The 3G Panorama will give you a clear sense of where you stand now and what to focus on improving. It gives new and important insights into your unique lens on the world, and how it affects all that you say and do.

TIPS:

- Focus matters. Allow ten minutes of uninterrupted time to complete the 3G Panorama to get the most useful results. It moves quickly.
- You get two shots. With your private link, you can complete the 3G Panorama one additional time, sometime in the future, to see how much you have improved after putting into practice the mindset-building tools provided later in this book.

Getting the Most from Your 3G Panorama Results

The comments we provide in this section are more about substance than about specific numbers. For detailed numbers, your feedback report will provide you with the most up-to-date statistics (ranges, means and more) based on the growing mass of people completing the 3G Panorama worldwide.

3G Total Score

The first score you want to look at is your 3G "barometer". Scores can range from 300 to 1,500, and the global average is 900. Scores follow the distribution in the following chart:

3G TOTAL SCORE DISTRIBUTION

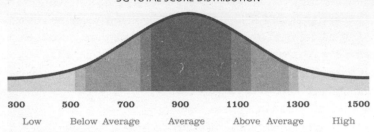

300	500	700	900	1100	1300	1500
Low	Below Average		Average	Above Average		High

The higher your score, the stronger your overall 3G Mindset. If your score is lower than you hoped, take heart! We will provide a number of tools in later chapters that can dramatically strengthen your 3G Mindset. Even if your 3G score is high, that doesn't mean you have been taking full advantage of it. A high score does not guarantee that you have been doing an effective job of *using* your mindset. We have tools to help you improve in that area as well.

The next step is to separate the 3Gs, and look at them individually. Scores for each G range from 100 to 500, with an average score of 300.

Global Score

Your Global Mindset is the vantage point of the 3G Mindset. It is all about your openness to new experiences and new ideas and your ability to make new connections on a global scale.

This aspect of your mindset is often underestimated. Depending on the job you have or strive for, it might be natural to think, "My job is here, not somewhere out there. Why focus on global, when good and grit apply *everywhere*?" The truth is that this element applies absolutely everywhere, and has become more and more important over time.

What was once a "nice-to-have" for a fringe minority who conducted global business has become a requirement for *anyone* working anywhere. If you question this statement, ask yourself these questions:

- If geographic boundaries were no issue, who could compete for and potentially do my job for less money?
- Who would love to take my desired job, and probably work even harder than I do?
- If I wanted to do any job better and faster, whom could I seek out, beyond my immediate work area, who could be the biggest help?
- How well do I reach beyond my assumed boundaries to get the best solutions to any problem I face?
- In what way does what I want to do or currently do connect with and play a role in the global economy?

Your score in this category is not necessarily age related. There are plenty of younger people, some of them among the up-and-comers or builders, who can't help but think globally in all they do, naturally scoring higher. It is the only world they know. But there are others who score surprisingly low. Likewise, there are older, more mature workers who are more likely to be found among the builders or finishers, who score among the highest on global. The key thing to remember is that global matters and, the higher your score, the better.

Begin with your overall global score. The higher you score on global, the more naturally you consider the questions above in all you do. People with high global scores automatically think beyond the immediate, obvious borders, reach out and tap people, resources and perspectives well beyond their sphere. They are more open, adaptable and curious, and are more inclined to use whatever technology or means are available to connect with a world way beyond traditional boundaries and borders.

This gives them a better-rounded perspective and helps them access more diverse, and often superior, solutions to everyday problems.

If you have a low global score, you may be missing out on tremendous opportunities, resources and options. The lower you score, the less connected you are in comparison to others, the more limited your perspective may be, the more blind you may be to the true competition for the best jobs, the less you may learn and the less value you may ultimately offer your employer.

What range are you in now? How might things be different if you had an even more Global Mindset? How happy are you with your current score? How might your work prospects improve if your global score went up?

Let's zoom in and look at the two clusters within the Global Mindset, starting with connectivity.

GLOBAL: CONNECTIVITY

This first global cluster is about the big picture. It describes how well you consider the broader, grander context and unintentional effects your decisions and behaviours may have. How well do you understand and appreciate the big picture or how your job, no matter how small it may seem, plays into and connects with the global marketplace?

How much do you let proximity limit your perspective? Do you naturally default to accessing ideas and resources in your immediate surroundings? Do you think, "Out of sight, out of mind"? Or do you regularly consider and connect with resources beyond your immediate world? If so, this enhances your perspective, effectiveness and potential value.

To what extent do you take advantage of technology and the Internet to go way beyond your immediate reality to access information, resources and solutions that you would otherwise never find? A lower score for global might suggest taking poor advantage of what the boundaryless world of technology can provide. A higher score indicates you are already tapped in and connected and you have probably benefited tremendously from what the grander world can provide.

GLOBAL: OPENNESS

Openness, flexibility and adaptability are among the mindset qualities employers desire most. It's important to take an honest look at how limited or boundaryless your mindset may be. The higher your global score, the more open you are to diverse points of view and to totally new ideas that may lead you to think and act differently. It is likely that you are naturally curious and you ask a lot of questions to ensure that you have considered all the options available to you. Your openness to innovations, opposing points of view and change can enhance your effectiveness.

The lower you score on global, the more closed-minded you may appear. You may tend to favour the first solution that you come up with, or shy away from change because it would involve more effort than usual. Improving your global score is a great way to accelerate your options and results. You know that person who is full of ideas and can connect with almost anyone anywhere? Chances are he or she scores high on global. And when it comes to getting the best jobs, global plays bigger than ever.

Microchallenge:
Global

1

Print your full online 3G Panorama report and circle the words in the global section of the 3G Mindset overview table that you most value, the ones that serve you best.

2

Put a star next to the two or three words or phrases that concern you most, those you most want to improve.

3

Now imagine how you will benefit by shrinking your weak spots and growing your strengths on global ever further.

Good Score

Good is the bedrock upon which the rest of your 3G Mindset is built. It is about seeing and engaging with the world in a way that truly benefits you and those around you.

Mindset is about how you see things, not about who you are. In other words, your good scores are not necessarily a gauge of whether or not you are a good *person*. They are a gauge of how good your mindset may be. But the stronger your good score is, the more natural it is for you to be a good person in a broad range of situations.

Character is timeless, but it is also a headline-level priority. It has become increasingly clear that a person can be perfectly competent, even extremely intelligent, but lack the basic Good Mindset it takes to earn our trust, respect and loyalty. This is one reason why employers care so much about hiring, keeping and promoting people who have a Good Mindset. Good is truly valued.

———

Look at your overall good score. The higher it is, the more of the good-related desirable qualities you're likely to have and to show. The lower it is, the less of them you naturally demonstrate.

The average good score is 300. If you score below average, you have a powerful opportunity for improvement. It means whatever success you have enjoyed up to now has been in spite of, not because of, this element of your 3G Mindset. You have the opportunity to make a quantum leap forward as you improve this dimension.

Whatever range you fall within, imagine how you and your life will be different as you significantly improve on good. How will it affect the way people relate to you, seek you out and their desire to include you in what they do? How will it affect the way you come across in a job interview, performance appraisal or the daily interactions that lead to success at work and in life? The benefits can be immense.

Let's zoom in a bit closer and consider two general clusters that make up your Good Mindset to help you better understand your good score.

GOOD: INTEGRITY

This cluster describes your moral foundation, your ethical perspective. It gives a sense of how grounded you are in the things that people think of when they talk about character—the timeless virtues that great thinkers have been extolling for more than two thousand years.

During big chunks of history, societies were grounded in very strict codes of conduct, moral doctrine determined by religion, law, or both. During the most recent decades, those absolutes have given way in many societies to what's called moral relativism, which is a fancy way of saying that when it comes to issues of right and wrong, more people see the answer as "it depends".

This kind of mindset offers more freedom but also opens the can of worms to moral ambiguity, where people think, "I'm not sure, so I'll do what I want." This may work well in isolated situations, but there is a strong case for the argument that the larger an employer is, the more defined and firm its moral code needs to be, and the more its employees need to adhere to it.

Make no mistake. Employers seek people with integrity who are grounded. We've never heard an employer say, "I wish I could find more morally weak people" (although we have seen exceptions where they seek greedy people who put wealth creation for a select few above any other cause, and expect their people to do whatever it takes to pursue it).

Mindset qualities such as honesty, trustworthiness, loyalty, authenticity, dependability and sincere helpfulness contribute to your overall good score.

GOOD: KINDNESS

This cluster is hugely important. It includes kindness, respect, fairness, compassion, empathy, generosity, humility and more. Lacking these qualities can be severely damaging to one's career and quality of life. Growing them can be enriching in both settings. The higher you score on good, the more of these rich traits you are likely to exhibit.

This cluster describes those facets of you that many employers remember, and some value most. It's pretty tough to make a case for retaining, let alone promoting, anyone who lacks these vital qualities. But those who are in the upper ranges can really stand out.

Microchallenge:
Good

1 Circle the words in the good section of the 3G Mindset overview table that you most value, the ones that serve you best. These have, most likely, been huge assets for you throughout your life. Take note of them. You will want to keep these "friends" close and highlight them as you build your 3G Mindset even further, and put these to use both at work and in life.

2 Put a star next to the two or three words or phrases that concern you most, those you most want to improve. Of these, which one(s) surprise or disturb you the most?

3 Now, imagine how you will benefit by shrinking your weak spots and growing your strengths on good ever further.

Grit Score

Grit is the fuel cell of your 3G Mindset. It is about approaching the world with the tenacity, resilience and relentlessness to come out ahead, regardless of your advantages or disadvantages in life.

Grit is that element of the 3G Mindset that describes your tenacity, perseverance, agility, capacity, energy and ability to scrap and scrape to make the impossible possible. It is that inner determination and fortitude, propelled by your hard-wired pattern of response to adversity.

Grit predicts and drives a wide range of the qualities that employers declare to be highly desirable factors in anyone they hire, such as commitment, accountability and determination. Beyond those quoted by the employers we spoke to, grit also drives optimism, happiness, health, innovation, performance, productivity, stamina, problem solving, calm, entrepreneurship, how quickly you are promoted and potential wealth, or how much money you make. Add this to the fact that most employers face more uncertainty, complexity, pressure and change, and you can see why they consider grit so absolutely essential.

Building greater grit alone has the potential to make you a dramatically more effective and successful person. It often separates those who fail from those who prevail. But when combined with global and good, grit realizes its full potential. Grit is also the element that determines how effectively you bring the other two Gs to life, when it matters most.

———

Look at your overall grit score. Again, a score of 300 is average. If your overall grit score is below average, any success you have had has required you to suffer unnecessarily. It has been tougher and more gruelling to achieve what you have than it has to be. It can be easier.

If, like many people, you score in the average range, then your grit has probably been helpful to you along the way but has plenty of room for improvement.

If you score in the upper ranges, then your grit has probably served you well most of the time. It has probably played a significant role in whatever successes you have enjoyed so far. And like any facet of the 3G Mindset, it can, most likely, be even stronger.

No matter what range you are in now, imagine how you will benefit as your grit grows stronger. How might it affect your stress, energy, resolve, capacity, perseverance and tenacity? Can you see how having more grit might fuel even greater success in getting and keeping the best job, now and for years to come?

Global and good each featured two clusters of qualities that when combined form a stronger construct. Grit is a bit more complex; growth, resilience, intensity, and tenacity are the four components that form (and conveniently spell) GRIT. Each one is important in its own way. And when you are able to put all four together, you can form bulletproof grit.

Zoom in and consider the four components of grit.

GRIT: GROWTH

This facet of mindset was best substantiated by Carol Dweck of Stanford University. Through her pioneering work with children, she proved that even tremendously talented kids with a "fixed" mindset fare and perform far worse than those with a "growth" mindset, one based on the assumption that through learning and effort one improves. The same applies to adults. People who walk around with fixed labels, such as "I'm smart" or "I'm creative", tend to do worse and improve less than those whose mindset feeds the belief, "I can do better if I apply myself."

The higher you score on grit, the more growth minded you may tend to be, and the more likely you are to see setbacks and failures as temporary, fixable and learning moments. The lower you score, the more likely you are to view setbacks as a threat to your sense of self, making them more serious, demoralizing and enduring. This is why a growth mindset strengthens your grit, and a fixed mindset makes you more vulnerable to life's challenges. The good news is that, no matter what your score, you can improve, and the benefits will be both noticeable and significant!

GRIT: RESILIENCE

It would be an understatement to say resilience has become a big deal. As the world gets more complex, chaotic, demanding, fast and difficult, resilience has really moved to the forefront of people's consciousness, and to the top of many employers' mindset priority lists. But tremendous grit without a solid dose of good and global can become a problem.

Your capacity to respond effectively to adversity—to be strengthened and improved by it—is arguably the central element of human endeavour, or all you do. Paul has spent decades pioneering and teaching the AQ (Adversity Quotient) theory and method, which is the most widely adopted approach worldwide for measuring and strengthening human resilience. Businesses across all industries and hundreds of thousands of people have used AQ to create real gains both within and beyond the workplace. The evidence is clear. Resilience is both foundational and essential.

However, as many employers intuitively conclude, we believe resilience, even grit, by itself is incomplete, even dangerous, without the counterbalance of the other two Gs.

If you score high on grit and tend to be resilient, that's great. You probably enjoy a lot of benefits, including people seeking you out when the going gets tough. If you score low, take heart. You can improve quickly and substantially, with huge rewards. As your grit and resilience improve, your burdens shrink, your stress level plummets and your quality of life soars.

GRIT: INTENSITY

This component of grit speaks to focus, discipline and energy. In some ways it is the opposite of apathy and attention deficit. Intensity describes your capacity to be fully engaged, immersed, if not enthralled in your tasks, in spite of whatever tempting distractions bombard you. As the world gets noisier and the number of distractions multiplies, the premium that employers place on the rare person who can demonstrate true intensity only grows. For them it's like finding the last rays of sunshine in a fluorescent-lit world.

Nicholas Carr wrote about the many distractions we face in everyday life in his book *The Shallows,* where he suggested that the internet was to blame for many of these distractions. He said, "What the Net seems to be doing is chipping away at my capacity for concentration and contemplation. Whether I'm online or not, my mind now expects to take in information the way the Net distributes it: in a swiftly moving stream of particles. Once I was a scuba diver in the sea of words. Now I zip along the surface like a guy on a jet ski."

He goes on to quote David Meyer, a neuroscientist at the University of Michigan and one of the leading experts on multitasking, who says, "We may overcome some of the inefficiencies inherent in multitasking but, except in rare circumstances, you can train until you're blue in the face and you'd never be as good as if you just focused on one thing at a time."

The higher you score on grit, the more naturally and fully you can focus on whatever you do, when others simply cannot or do not. It also means you are probably more disciplined than most people, staying engaged and seeing projects through to their finish, even if they get relatively dull as time goes on. You can shut out external distractions better than most, which helps you to be far more productive and produce higher quality outcomes in whatever you do.

The lower you score on grit, the more the opposite is true and the more easily you fall prey to distractions and let your attention flit around. This reduces your productivity and it shrinks your effectiveness, since few tasks that are the least bit challenging can be done masterfully without a reasonable dose of intensity. And, even if they can, they can be done even better when intensity is turned up.

GRIT: TENACITY

Imagine how hard you would work, how far you would go and what you would sacrifice to get the one thing in life that matters to you more than anything else. That surge you feel inside, the steely resolve, is tenacity. Tenacity comprises one part perseverance and one part sheer effort. It is the "never give up" element so desperately needed as the tasks, changes, and challenges employers deal with become more and more complex. Like all facets of your 3G Mindset, tenacity has become more important, more in demand and arguably more difficult to find in the people employers hire, keep and advance.

The higher you score on grit, the more likely you are to stick to and stick with your commitments, even in the face of real adversity. And adversity is the true test of your tenacity and grit. Like many facets of your mindset, it is in the moments of adversity when your tenacity matters most. If you want to truly stand apart in an employer's eyes and memory, there are few more dramatic ways than to be the one who pushes forward when everyone else gives up. The farmer who keeps his hand firmly on the plow and trudges through the most miles of mud reaps the biggest harvest.

People with lower grit scores may put forth effort until it gets too tough, then give up or give reasons and excuses for not completing something rather than proving they can finish the task. This sort of response to the tough stuff is common but not terribly effective or attractive to employers. When you give up, it tends to make you feel worse about yourself as the suspicion that you may have disappointed others grows. This is why employing the tools offered in the next chapters will give you a genuine edge as you improve your tenacity, productivity, effectiveness and value in the eyes of any employer.

Microchallenge:
Grit

 Circle the words in the grit section of the 3G Mindset overview table that you most value, the ones that serve you best.

2

Put a star next to the two or three words or phrases that concern you most, those you most want to improve.

3

Now imagine how you will benefit by shrinking your weak spots and growing your strengths on grit ever further.

It's important to think beyond your scores and consider how 3G can shape your career, even your entire life, because wake-up calls come when we least expect them. And when they do, they can change our lives. Sometimes they threaten to destroy everything we work for, or simply throw our plans out the window. But with the 3Gs all working together, you can start with nothing and make a powerful mark in the world.

3G applies with equal force and with equal power to determine your success when you go for your very first job. And even high-powered top executives have to start somewhere.

THE REAL STORY—3G MINDSET AT WORK

Mike Crosby was twenty-one years old and a junior in college when his fiancée, Laura, got pregnant. In an instant their focus shifted from "Where's tonight's party?" to "How the heck are we going to pay this month's bills?" We picked Mike's story (among many) because it touches all the clusters and qualities that make up the 3Gs, showing what can happen when you really put your mindset to work.

"I don't think I even knew what a CV was, but I knew I had better go out and get a real job, and fast!" Mike recalls as he describes that moment of truth. "To make matters worse the economy was in the tank, and every job I applied for was completely besieged with applicants far more qualified than I was. It was pathetic!"

But Mike had grit. He got intense, he persevered and he kept trying new approaches to land worse and worse jobs, farther and farther from home, with only a growing list of rejections to show for his efforts. He refused to give up. Rather than having no job, Mike took the only job he could find, and the one he thought he'd never do.

He became a prison guard. According to Mike, "It's the one job that always seems to have openings, so I did what I could. It wasn't exactly a career move, but it wasn't that bad . . . At least I met some really interesting people from a side of society I never knew. Besides, being six foot seven has its advantages."

Being a prison guard is listed as one of the fifty worst jobs in the United States. No surprise. One reason? It's considered a dead end. So, where does a full-time prison guard in a dead-end job, with a pregnant wife and no money end up? How about CEO of a company that reinvented the way one of the largest industries in the world serves its customers? Mike got there by putting his 3G Mindset to work in every job he took as he struggled and ascended the ranks of the corporate world—taking on an ever-increasing range of responsibilities—with uncommon speed. Mindset is what sets Mike apart.

One reason that Mike stands out is because of his tremendous grit. In fact, he scores in the top 3 per cent. He has this great knack for making the impossible possible. He thrives on challenges when credible "advisers" tell him that something exciting simply can't be done. Then he goes and does it. Big stuff like leading his recent company, Irving Oil, to dramatically *grow* customer loyalty, market share and profitability immediately after Hurricane Katrina, when all of his competitors sagged and the media was trashing Big Oil for gouging their customers. "Why survive adversity when you can *harness* it?" That's one of his favourites.

Mike often gets asked, "So how'd you get from there to *here*?" The problem is that that's the wrong question. The right question is *"What does it take inside anyone* [like you and me] *to start at the bottom, beat the odds, and really make a mark?"*

At first glance, you might mistake Mike Crosby, even when he puts on a fancy suit, for just a good-natured, "normal" guy. In fact, that's exactly what he considers himself to be. Nothing more. Chances are, like most folks, you would really like him. You'd trust him. You'd learn to rely on him. He's the kind of guy you would want to invite over for a barbecue, sit next to on the plane or have on your team. He's the kind of guy you confide in, believe and appreciate.

But knowing what you now know, you realize this all goes well beyond being likeable or a great guy. If you were to score Mike Crosby on another G, good, again, he'd be in the top 3 per cent. According to those who work with and for him, as well as the people outside his work, Mike pretty much exemplifies each of the qualities that comprise integrity and kindness. He repeatedly takes the hard hits for taking the tough stands on treating people right, even when he's under immense pressure not to. If forced to lie, he would simply resign. And it's important to point out that being with Mike isn't like inviting the pope over for dinner. It's easy to be perfectly comfortable being yourself around Mike.

Okay, so he's glowing with good and grit. What about global? Fair question. Mike ran his latest business out of Concord, New Hampshire, a quaint, provincial town. It's the kind of place people intentionally move to in an attempt to keep life simple. And Mike's a New England guy. He was raised there, educated there, works there, played sports there and raises his family there. His whole world is New England. It'd be easy for him to be provincial.

But when interviewed in the context of his recent job in the energy industry, Mike admitted he makes and implements micro-decisions based on macrofactors in order to grow the business and help his people secure their futures. "When the Arabs cut production, or some foreign tyrant makes a threat, I've got to immediately factor in how that might affect my neighbour's home heating oil, and what we need to do next." In fact, Mike scores in the top 3 per cent on global too.

This sort of rare, global perspective has helped Mike land and be promoted (usually over older, more experienced people) within every job he's ever held. He gets the big picture. People learn to count on him for that. This mindset also helped him generate billions in value for his employer. Not bad for a prison guard.

The point of this story is not to repulse you with a perfect example. In fact, we had to promise Mike adamantly that that wasn't the case before he even approved our sharing his story. The point is to share with you the story of a very real, down-to-earth, likeable person who, amid others with fancier degrees, more years and more qualifications, has used his 3G Mindset to forge a remarkable career and life. And we fervently believe that, when it comes to putting mindset to work, what one person can do, many can do, including you.

Earlier in the book we pointed out that 3G applies from the CEO on down, at any level, for any job and at any stage in your career. Many of the unsung heroes of business, like Mike Crosby, started humbly searching for a foothold, without any special advantages or help, and used their 3G Mindset to build an exceptionally admirable career and life. No matter where you are in your career, from "not yet begun" to "as high as it gets", 3G will determine how far you get and how much you enjoy yourself along the way.

3G and Gen G

You can and may already have begun to picture how your 3G Mindset (and results) plays out differently based on your current career stage. For **up-and-comers**, global may be more assumed, but that does not mean it is optimized. If you are in the front end of your career, it is safe to say that your Global Mindset will determine the opportunities you consider and enjoy. Those who limit their horizons tend to enjoy more limited opportunities and careers. Those who can see and actively reach past the horizon enjoy a far richer assortment and bounty of ideas, connections, relationships, opportunities and experiences.

Good will determine how you treat and are perceived by others over time, which will determine whether your menu of opportunities grows or shrinks. Grit is what it takes to relentlessly pursue or create those opportunities no one else will.

If you are a **builder**, global matters, but grit and good weave together in a particularly profound way. Demonstrating the good qualities, especially in the moments of truth, sets you apart from others. Using your grit to let your good shine is one of the signs of greatness, and it tends to get you noticed for those next-level opportunities.

As a **finisher** nearer to the end of your career, it is easy to set global aside. That would be a mistake. Having that long, far-reaching view of your role, impact and legacy, when combined with your good and grit, will guide you to make the kind of decisions that help you finish strong. The best and most fulfilled finishers are those who weave 3G together in everything they do.

Profiling Your 3G

With Mike's example in mind, take a look at the shape of your 3G profile. Is it perfectly shaped or lopsided? The more lopsided it is, the clearer the message that you need to focus on a specific area of your 3G Mindset— either global, good or grit—more than the others. If it is fairly balanced, that means you will get the biggest gains from focusing on specific facets inside one or more of the 3Gs.

SAMPLE 3G PROFILES

Most people have some imbalance. Some have extreme imbalance, where one lobe or area of their profile is dramatically larger than the other two. So don't be disturbed if yours is out of whack. The purpose is to give you clarity on how to round it out, so your entire mindset works to your advantage.

Your short-term goal is to make some strong strides, some initial clear improvement in the specific area(s) you choose. Your long-term goal is to score well above average on the individual and combined elements of the 3G Panorama, to have the kind of mindset that sets you apart and that employers most desire.

How do you decide where to begin? Here's our suggestion. Forget the numbers for a minute. Go with your gut. Of all the comments or facets of global, good and grit, which, if any, upset you the most? Which one(s) really bother you? Chances are these hit on a key priority or deep, personal value. That means they deserve your attention and effort first. Or of them all, which one(s) excite you the most to improve? If you could improve two or three, which dimensions would you pick that would offer you the most dramatic benefits? That's probably a great place to start.

In some ways this chapter is the toughest. It's full of information and new insights. You could spend as much or as little time on your 3G Panorama feedback report as you like. But our advice is don't just set it down and forget about it. Revisit your results frequently. Use it as your guide, inspiration and pathway to developing a more enriching 3G Mindset that you will be able to apply both inside and outside work. The more you do, the more you'll learn. Each time you look at your results, you'll discover something new and be able to apply it as you *Put Your Mindset to Work*.

- -

CHAPTER RECAP

The 3G Panorama Preview gives a brief glimpse of what your 3G Mindset might look like.

The 3G Panorama (www.3GMindset.com/book) is the most robust, complete way to gauge your 3G Mindset.

The 3G scores range from 300 to 1,500, with a mean of 900.

Each G (global, good, grit) has scores ranging from 100 to 500, with a mean of 300.

You can immediately begin to strengthen any and all facets of your 3G Mindset using the tools provided in the following chapters.

Global
has two clusters: connectivity and openness.

Good
has two clusters: integrity and kindness.

Grit
has four components: growth, resilience, intensity and tenacity.

- -

Now that you know your current 3G Mindset, you're ready to dig in and learn how to make each facet of your 3G Mindset even stronger and apply these new strengths to getting and keeping the best jobs, beginning with the next chapter. Each of the following chapters is chock-full of tools and tips and proven approaches for permanently improving your 3G Mindset. We will start by explaining a bit about the science behind mindset and the reasons you have the power to change it.

MASTER YOUR MINDSET: HOW IT ALL WORKS

If you hear a voice within you say "you cannot paint", then
by all means paint and that voice will be silenced.
– Vincent van Gogh

Let's start with the good news. You *can* improve. In fact, thanks to some of the most significant and relatively unknown scientific discoveries in recent decades, we now know, beyond a shadow of a doubt, that *you can measurably and permanently strengthen all facets of your 3G Mindset*. But you have to *want* to, and you have to work at it to really make it stick.

This chapter explains how it all works, so you can master your mindset faster and better. Some of what you are about to read may amaze you. Certainly, the more we learn about how this all works, the more amazed (and excited) we become too. And you don't have to be a scientist to understand it. Our basic premise is that the more you know about and can vividly picture what's happening inside your head, the faster and better you can reset (or simply tune up) your mindset.

If you want to dive right into the 3G Mindset-improving tools, you can certainly skip to the next chapter. There is also tremendous benefit in first knowing how it all works, so you can get the most from the remaining chapters.

Reset Your Mindset

It would take volumes to explain all the complex details of how the science behind your mindset works. So what we are about to provide you with is an oversimplification, and it is in no way meant to trivialize some serious pioneering research.

Let's face it. No one knows the full truth of how mindset works. With each new study, we learn even more. But what we have discovered provides a compelling case and explanation for how you can strengthen your mindset *permanently*. That much we *do* know. We're sure you will find the headlines as fascinating as we do.

We will provide the gist of how it works, so you can picture what you are about to do. Some of it sounds pretty scientific (it is), but the basic process is really pretty simple. First let's hit the science stuff.

The Science

To explain how mindset works, we're going to use some pretty technical terms, such as myelin, hard-wiring, neuroplasticity, genetic switches and mirror neurons. Don't worry—this will be relatively painless, and definitely worth the effort.

MYELIN

You probably know from experience that the outer coating on an electric wire protects you from fire and shock. But did you know that the thickness of that coating can determine the strength and distance of the connection? A similar thing happens inside those three precious pounds of matter between your ears. Your brain comprises a hundred billion cells (dendrites) with four trillion potential connections (synapses). These are big numbers.

Recently, Tim Berners-Lee, the creator of the World Wide Web, proclaimed that there are now more pages on the internet than there are cells in his brain. But this only happened at the end of the first decade of the twenty-first century. Before that, your brain cells far outnumbered the total number of internet pages worldwide. Difficult to imagine, we know, but true.

How do you form the best and strongest connections between your hundred billion brain cells with 4 trillion possible links? How do you form the ones that will serve you best in life? How do you avoid or, in effect, disconnect the ones that serve you poorly?

Think of it this way. How do you form the best and strongest connections with other people? There are nearly 7 billion people on our planet. That's nearly 7 billion potential friends. You form friendships based on several factors, including what they have to offer (utility and attraction), how close by they may work or live (proximity), which ones you see most often (frequency), and the strength and energy you put into your interactions (intensity).

These factors are like the coating on a wire. If you are really attracted to someone whom you see frequently and is close by, and you both put tremendous energy into every interaction, then you may form a "thick" or deep friendship and connection. If you are unattracted, far apart, see each other infrequently and don't put a lot of energy into the times you do spend together, then the friendship, or connection, is likely to be "thin" or weak.

In your brain, connections are formed for many of the same reasons and the strength, speed and intensity of those connections are dramatically affected by the coating on the wire, which is called myelin. The more focused and intense you are about a specific activity, thought or belief, the more myelin or coating you develop.

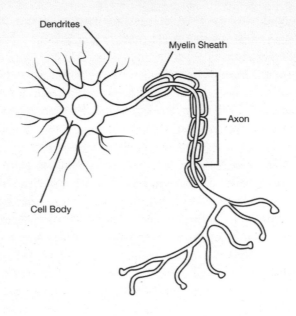

An illustration of a neuron showing the myelin
sheath around the axon within the brain.
Image courtesy of National Institutes of Health.

DEEP PRACTICE

If you have ever struggled to learn a new sport, musical instrument, words to a song or equation for science class, you have experienced what scientists call deliberate or "deep practice". Our understanding of deep practice comes from in-depth psychological research alongside intensive studies of how the best coaches in the world develop exceptional talent in sports, music and more.

Deep practice happens when you *intensely* focus on, struggle through, repeat and improve a specific behaviour, a defined pattern of thought or action. Practising like this creates more myelin layers. The deeper the practice, the faster and the thicker you form myelin, and the faster and stronger that connection becomes. More is better. And the struggle— that frustrating part that makes you want to throw up your arms and quit—is absolutely essential if you want thick, healthy myelin. If you do not struggle, you cannot get the full benefit of deep practice.

Think of that moment when an infant tries to stand. First she puts her hand up on the chair or table. Then with several seconds and perhaps many attempts of white-knuckle, body-quaking intensity, she wills her untrained limbs to stand. Chances are she flops straight back down on her bottom, but she just keeps on struggling back up.

Just like the infant learning to stand, you need to keep on pushing beyond your current limits for deep practice to work. Failing again and again is a vital part of your struggle to make it through to the next level. "No one is born with genius cells," says Swedish-born Anders Ericsson, now professor of psychology at Florida State University. Instead it is work like this, which actively "stimulates growth and the transformations of cells", that "creates the biochemical change in the brain to take you forward".

So the best way to get the most out of every skill and tool we bring you will be through deep practice. You can increase the efficiency of a given set of connections by *3,000 per cent*, simply through deep practice. That means you can make your new and better mindset natural, even automatic.

HARD-WIRING

Like seeing the image of an enemy or ally projected into the helm of a spaceship in a sci-fi movie, imagine a holographic projection inside your brain that forms your mindset. We have good reason to believe that almost like an array of tiny projectors, different connections of different intensities in effect illuminate and animate different pixels of your mindset, forming your unique lens through which you see and navigate life and all facets of your career.

You have facets of the 3G Mindset in place already. Some pixels clarify and contribute to its shining strength. Others blur or detract, perhaps to the point where the best parts are hard to spot. You want to dim the bad ones and add to the helpful ones so your 3G Mindset burns brightly.

Imagine that each pixel is fuelled by its connection to neighbouring neurons. No matter how good they are, you want ever-better ones. The process of laying down that new, improved pathway is often called "hard-wiring". It refers to what literally happens inside your brain.

If you have ever seen a dirt footpath that people use as a shortcut across two paved areas or as the diagonal shortcut across an otherwise nice lawn, you notice that the more it is used, the deeper and thicker it gets and the faster you can move along it. That's hard-wiring. Forming deliberate shortcuts that lead to superior performance is what we are going to help you do throughout the remainder of this book.

When Paul's sister Sabina was in her medical residency, she was blindsided in her small car by a delivery truck careening through a red light as she crossed the intersection. The resulting brain injury left her all but incapacitated. She did not respond to light or sound and could barely speak. Clearly, her aspirations of becoming a doctor were over. Or *were* they?

Through deliberate "deep practice" training by neurologists and real struggle, Sabina was able to perform a miracle that is now accepted medical therapy. She proved she could *hard-wire* and *myelinate* new pathways, going around the damaged tissue, to regain her speech and capabilities. She then continued her medical training and is now unlocking other mysteries of the mind as a respected psychiatrist.

NEUROPLASTICITY

The brain's miraculous capacity to reshape, reroute and rejuvenate as a result of experience is called "neuroplasticity". In reshaping and rejuvenating your mindset, you will use the same mechanism that enables old people to strengthen their memories, disabled people to grow new capabilities and blind people to "see" images through a device connected to their tongue. This will help you to deliberately abandon the less effective facets and grow new, more effective facets of your 3G Mindset.

Through neuroplasticity you can physically increase your brain's capacity. London black cab drivers provide just one example of how experience can change your brain. London is an ancient city that has never followed a grid plan. Its medieval streets twist and turn across one another, completely baffling outsiders. But if you hail a black cab drivers, he or she always knows how to reach your destination without even glancing at a map or a satellite image.

That's because to become a cabbie each driver has to gain "the Knowledge". On average it takes thirty-four months of hard work and twelve "appearances" in front of the ferocious examiners before anyone can successfully demonstrate that he has memorized the city-centre tangle of more than twenty-five thousand streets. James often catches sight of one of the trainees zipping around the corner of his office building on a little moped, practising the latest route to be learned with the directions pinned on to a clipboard fixed in front. Examiners like to test the drivers by asking them to drive routes between two places that are connected by a pun or a joke. For example, one of the examiners' favourite requests is "Take me from Warren Street to Rabbit Row."

But it took neurologist Eleanor Maguire and her colleagues from University College in London to discover the effect learning all this knowledge had on the cabbies' brains. With the help of MRI scanners they found that the brain area connected with spatial memory and learning (the hippocampus) is literally larger in London cabbies than in their control group of non-drivers. More important still, the longer a driver's career continued, the bigger this area became. It continues to grow through deep practice.

Cabbies just go on acquiring even more brain capacity as they gain more experience. This effect has now been identified in people who have mastered all kinds of expertise, from musicians to athletes. Even gaining a purely mental ability, such as meditation, actually changes the brain's internal functions and structures.

You, too, can grow your brain and your mindset. Your brain is extremely flexible and agile, well beyond what any of us ever dreamed possible, and you have the power to reshape and rejuvenate it.

GENETIC SWITCHES

But are there limitations? Aren't some facets of mindset at least partially genetic? The short answer is yes. Optimism and happiness, for example, appear to be at least partially, even significantly, genetic. That means that if you are a natural sourpuss, you may never be giddy with joy. But it does not mean you cannot become substantially happier, within your potential range.

Genes have always been thought of as fixed, like height. But even height, within a genetically determined range, is affected by how you are raised, what you eat and how healthy you are. That is why today, in China, we see a young generation that in many cases is an entire head taller than their parents.

In fact, a whole series of scientific advances has transformed our understanding of the impact genes have. In the 1920s, the founder of IQ tests, Lewis Terman, was convinced that everyone's abilities were fixed at birth. At the end of the last century academics seemed to believe that nearly two-thirds of our intelligence was directly inherited through unchangeable genes. Now, in the twenty-first century, as author David Shenk has explained, we know that's just not true. Quite simply, you have far more power to develop and change even your IQ than was thought possible just a few years ago.

Think of genes as dimmer switches on the wall. The switches you have or don't have are determined by your parents. Which ones get turned up or down, on or off, can be largely influenced by *you*. Just because you have a switch for adult onset diabetes doesn't mean it has to be activated.

As the emerging science of epigenetics—the study of how gene behaviour changes—tells us, you can dramatically reduce the chances of its being activated simply by altering your environment and taking great care of your health. The same thing can be said for any of the negative aspects of mindset. Even if you inherited the tendency for some, you can prevent or minimize most of them, most of the time. You can also deliberately turn up and build upon the good switches, those parts of your genetic cocktail that can prove beneficial.

The latest science goes even further. It turns out that your genes are far more dynamically influenced by the environment than was previously realized, turning on its head the centuries-old debate about the impact of nature versus nurture.

The old analysis assumes that your unique identity is created through the interplay of "genes plus environment" (G + E). Now we know that a far more dynamic development is at work, of "genes multiplied by environment" (G × E), which means that the impact of your environment can create a much bigger range of possible outcomes. The environment starts to affect which of your genes are switched on or off from the moment you are conceived. Astonishingly, the most recent research suggests that the environment affects you earlier still. What happens even before you are conceived can have a major impact on who you become.

How can this be? Another insight from the new science of epigenetics explains. The protein-rich chemical mix that surrounds and protects your genes (the epigenome) shifts profoundly in response to the multifaceted environment around us, and it is these changes that have the power to switch your genes on or off. Scientists have tracked the impact of a whole range of different environments, from stressful to stimulating. Numerous twenty-first-century experiments have conclusively proved that these environmentally induced changes can actually be inherited. This means that what happened to and around your parents influenced not just who they became but what they passed on to you. This can apply to anything from heart disease and glaucoma to happiness and laughter.

James has been told that his tendency to wheezy coughs as a child may have been a "genetic shadow" of the tuberculosis that affected much earlier generations of his family. Now we know that your emotional outlook as well as your physical characteristics can be directly affected by what has *happened* to your ancestors in the past, not just some preset genetic code they granted you upon birth. Their experiences can literally shape yours.

It is easy to underestimate just how important all this information is to our ability to determine our own future—and that of our children.

Carol Dweck, the psychology professor from Stanford University who has worked with children and young adults for four decades, has found that people naturally divide into two contrasting groups: those who think their intelligence is fixed and others who believe that, with effort, it can grow. You may recall that Dweck's growth dimension is a vital component of both your grit and your overall 3G Mindset.

But it also turns out that all those people with a fixed mindset are scientifically incorrect. Your talents are not fixed. While your genes don't change, their effects do. With effort you can develop your intelligence, and even transform the make-up of your brain. The "growth mindset" is the right way forward, as well as the most effective for you personally. You *can* grow your mindset, and people who follow this belief and path, Dweck's research confirms, are more successful as a direct result.

Western governments seeking to overcome the entitlement myths that have blighted their economies are catching on. In 2010, the US Department of Health and Human Services gave its first grant of more than $800,000 to help apply Professor Dweck's theories to teachers and educational leaders, the heart of the American school system. There's some argument that this is the long overdue corrective measure to the disastrous "self-esteem movement" that was prevalent in the 1980s and 1990s in the California school system, resulting in a significant percentage of kids with poor performance but such high self-esteem that they saw no reason to try harder. Ultimately, Dweck and Health and Human Services seek to change an entrenched mindset in the American school system.

All this is very good news. Your genes and your upbringing don't have to be your destiny. And the majority of your 3G Mindset is within your influence. You can literally hard-wire yourself to employ the mindset you want, to gain and keep the best jobs and the best life.

PEOPLE MAKE THE DIFFERENCE

You can begin this journey right now, by yourself. But you don't have to do this alone. In fact, the latest science shows that you need others, especially when forming specific facets of a 3G Mindset. It also reveals that you are far more influenced by the people around you than you might realize.

Within your environment other people have by far the biggest effect on you. Whether you know it or not, your fellow humans have the most direct power to change the way you think, feel and act.

Your biological make-up programmes you to absorb and copy other people, automatically. Not only are you biologically hard-wired to mimic how other people look—in copying what the experts call "outward displays"—you actually take on the feelings that go with them in an effect known technically as "affective afference", or the facial feedback theory.

We will briefly explain the science here, so you can picture how this amazing mechanism plays out, especially when strengthening the good-related qualities of your mindset, since those involve your disposition towards and with others. However, this science applies to all three Gs. Through the remainder of this book and beyond, we invite you to consider how this natural ability to co-experience with others can enrich your relationships and your life.

Brain scans show that when people are asked to imitate an angry expression, the area of their brains responsible for registering emotions lights up. Your skin and facial muscle movements play a big part in directly transmitting these emotions, as neurologist Andreas Hennenlotter proved when his volunteers agreed to have the frown muscles on their faces frozen with Botox injections. Without being able to physically lower their brows or scrunch up their faces in rage, the brain impact of copying angry expressions was drastically reduced. Given your natural tendency to imitate the emotional expressions you see in people around you, you simply can't help but "catch" their feelings. In this sense, mindset can be contagious!

What's more, neurologists have now confirmed that your brain is full of mirror neurons, which automatically fire when you simply observe others doing something. If you watch a football game on TV, for instance, the areas of the brain associated with the physical actions of kicking and running light up in empathy with what you see.

According to Professor Giacomo Rizzolatti and his colleagues at Italy's University of Palma, mirror neurons help explain how empathy works. They give you direct understanding of the emotions of others, completely bypassing any need to think things through consciously.

These responses are fine-tuned to extract subtly different meanings *instantly,* before your conscious mind can ponder the implications.

When you see someone smiling, the part of your brain responsible for your own happy facial expressions will light up. When a similar-looking expression is actually a grimace of shock, the brain automatically registers the difference. A new set of mirror neurons will fire in response as you literally experience the other person's pain.

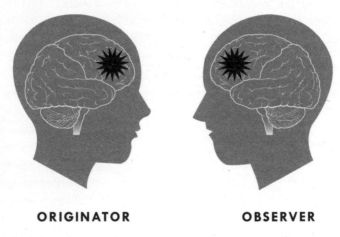

ORIGINATOR   **OBSERVER**

Simplified illustration of mirror cells.

SITUATIONAL FORCES

Brain chemistry is not the only reason why others influence you. The impact of people's behaviour should never be underestimated. So-called situational forces are strong enough to turn ordinary human beings to incomprehensible evil, as social psychologist Philip Zimbardo found out when he set up his famous Stanford Prison Experiment in 1971. Professor Zimbardo went on to study how situational forces turned family-loving Europeans into Nazi exterminators and, more recently, idealistic young American soldiers into degrading torturers within Iraq's Abu Ghraib prison.

Fortunately, situational forces can also be supremely positive and help you achieve far more than you could by yourself. "Clusters" or "hubs" of influence nurture outstanding talent. The extraordinary technological leaps forward towards the end of the twentieth century were born out of the creative ferment of California's Silicon Valley, just as fantastic art from Leonardo, Michelangelo and a host of others emerged from the creative cauldron of sixteenth-century Renaissance Italy. Intense competition, communities of passionate interest and the lively cross-fertilization of ideas can all help you go further than you ever could alone.

So what does this mean for you and your 3G Mindset? The words of John Donne, the seventeenth-century British poet and preacher, that "no man is an island, entire of itself" turn out to be literally true. How you feel, what you do and your physical make-up right down to the chemistry in your brain are programmed to be directly influenced by others.

This has huge implications for you. Research shows that whatever your goal, whether it is to lose weight or gain a dream job, you will be more successful in reaching it if you are surrounded by a support group of other people on the same path.

So invite your friends to help, create new networks, intentionally surround yourself with people who possess mindsets you respect and wish to emulate. Then find ways in which you can join in to support one another and travel the 3G journey together. Or compete against these people to intensify your deep practice. But also build relationships with them to help your whole body and your brain automatically absorb their approach.

A huge range of sciences has come together—from neuroscience and behavioural economics to biological, social and developmental psychology—to reveal just how much ability you have to transform your own mindset. Yet there is one further major science that can propel you further towards the future you want.

The Science of Motivation

Scientists have now identified three main drivers of motivation. The first two have been known for centuries. **Behavioural motivation** comes from within, from your biological needs, for instance, for food or shelter or to find a mate. Your basic survival needs always have to be met first before other kinds of motivation can have any impact.

The second driver, **external motivation**, comes from outside yourself, from external rewards. Understanding external drives can enormously help you steer your mindset journey to success. Psychologist and behavioural scientist Dan Ariely tells a very personal story about how this worked for him.

Eight years after recovering from a horrific high school accident that left him with third-degree burns over 70 per cent of his body, the liver disease that Dan had picked up in an early infected blood transfusion was at last diagnosed as hepatitis C. The good news was that a new treatment was just beginning to go on trial. The bad news was that this involved self-injecting a drug called Interferon three times a week and enduring horrible aftereffects each time, including sixteen-hour bouts of high fever, nausea, headaches and vomiting.

These injections had to be continued, week in and week out, for a year and a half. After eighteen months, Dan learned that his treatment had been successful, but also that—understandably—not one other patient in the protocol had been able to keep to this highly unpleasant regime.

So what made Dan different? Young as he was, Dan realized that willpower and self-control alone would never get him through the eighteen-month trial. Instead he decided to motivate himself with something he really loved: the movies.

On the morning of each Monday, Wednesday and Thursday when Dan's injections were due, he picked out a whole bunch of new films and spent the entire day focused on just how much he was looking forward to watching them. Immediately after his evening injection, surrounded by all the blankets and buckets he needed to cope with its horrible aftereffects, he started up his own personal film show. Tricking his brain to associate the act of the injection with the rewarding experience of watching some fantastic movies gave him the motivation he needed to make it through.

You can make the most of external motivation too. As you embark on your 3G Mindset journey, consider rewarding your efforts along the way with something you love—whether it's the chance to watch your favourite film, toss a ball with your child or pet, or indulge in a taste of your favourite chocolate.

But you also have a third motivational driver to help build your 3G Mindset. Too often ignored, **intrinsic motivation** can become your most vital support.

It sounds so simple. Intrinsic motivation influences you to do something for its own sake, rather than because you expect to gain from it.

Yet astonishingly it turns out that intrinsic motivation can be a far more effective motivator than the biggest financial prize you could imagine.

Although some bankers still find this difficult to accept, the latest research proves that dangling enormous rewards in front of people does not make them perform better. If anything, it makes them perform worse.

In one recent major study, people were promised the equivalent of a day's, a week's or five months' pay if they performed well in a series of games and tasks. (Before you ask how you can join in, this experiment took place in India, where the cost of living is lower, so the researchers could afford it.) What happened? According to Professor Dan Ariely, "the low- and medium-bonus groups performed the same. The big-bonus group performed worst of all."

The same effect has been proved again and again around the world. In 2009, Professor Sam Bowles from the Santa Fe Institute analysed fifty-one separate experimental studies of financial incentives in employment relations. The prestigious London School of Economics (which jointly hosted the British launch of the research with two other UK universities) said the study showed "overwhelming evidence that these incentives may reduce an employee's natural inclination to complete a task and derive pleasure from doing so".

And that's the point. While external carrots and sticks undeniably help people achieve in the short term, it is your own natural inclination, your intrinsic motivation, that is the most powerful force in the long term.

Many hundreds of experiments have examined a whole range of situations—from children at play to creative artists at work—and reached the same scholarly conclusions. Whenever people take on something for its own intrinsic challenge and interest, rather than for an external reward, they are more creative, effective and successful as a result.

The implications for you are huge. In Ancient Greece, Aristotle identified that human beings had one ultimate goal: to be happy. Scientists claim that exploring the effects of intrinsic motivation offers the solution to this eternal quest.

Have you ever lost yourself in doing something, completely absorbed in it, whether mastering a musical instrument, icing a cake, printing photos in a darkroom, or stripping down a car engine and building it up again?

More than two thousand years ago, Taoist master Chuang-Tzu identified this kind of joyous total absorption as the mystical state of *yu*. Modern-day psychologist Mihaly Csikszentmihalyi explains, "Yu refers to the right way of following the path or Tao . . . Yu is the way Chuang-Tzu believes people should live—without concern for external rewards, spontaneously and with full commitment."

The mystical heights of *yu* are not reserved for the rich or powerful. Meeting the challenges of everyday tasks and perfectly applying the expertise you have developed is achievable by all of us. The best moments of all, Csikszentmihalyi has found, usually occur when a person's mind is stretched to its limits in a voluntary effort to accomplish something difficult and worthwhile, with intrinsic motivation at its core. This he calls "optimal experience".

The state of *yu* can be achieved when people are wholly engaged in what they are doing, delighting in their ability to overcome challenges and at one with the task they have in hand.

Having a long-term goal in mind can transform your prospects for success. In 1997, Gary McPherson (now a professor and head of music at Melbourne University) studied the musical development of 157 randomly selected children. He was intrigued by the difference between those whose musical development shot ahead in the first nine months, against those who quickly started to fall behind. One by one he tested for a whole range of variables, from IQ to aural sensitivity to income level, only to eliminate each one. The real difference, it turned out, came from answers to a simple question asked at the start of the study, which was simply "How long do you plan to play?"

Gary ranked the answers into the three categories of short-term, medium-term and long-term commitment. He plotted these on a graph against each child's progress. To his astonishment, the child's commitment before he even started his first lesson had far more impact on his progress than practising for longer. (Remember: it is not how many hours you spend, it is how intensely and deeply you practice that makes the difference.) In fact, the long-term committed outperformed the short-term committed by an astonishing 400 per cent.

So here are some of the key drivers of intrinsic motivation, each one of which can inspire and support you as you develop your 3G Mindset. As you read each description, think about how that particular motivator has played out in the moments and tasks where you have felt most naturally and fully engaged.

AUTONOMY

You feel most motivated when your actions are self-determined and you feel in control. The offer of a reward can actually result in a loss of engagement. Children absorbed in a game will lose interest if they are told it is part of their homework. Artists spend longer amounts of time on work they conceive themselves than when they have a commission, no matter how lucrative it is. So when and where possible, set your own long-term objectives, decide on your own pace and relish your sense of control over yourself and your future as you pursue the right mindset.

MASTERY

The interest and excitement of putting your skills into practice, facing up to adversity and overcoming obstacles to reach a deep understanding of what you are doing is one of the most motivating forces of all. Demonstrating grit as you grow it, for example, is typically highly rewarding, whereas rewards such as grades or stars or big cash sums actually limit your ambition and your efforts. According to intrinsic motivation expert Daniel Pink and key researchers including professors Edward Deci and Richard Ryan from the University of Rochester in New York, carrot-and-stick motivation can work, short term, but it is astonishing to see how completely many of the classic rewards can backfire. Aim for mastery to achieve your dreams and maximize your enjoyment of the journey. We must struggle for mastery. Remove the struggle and our motivation can plummet.

CONNECTION WITH OTHERS

Human beings are social animals, and we have an innate drive to relate to others and the world about us. Remember: mindset feeds mindset. Rather than surrounding yourself with people who tend to settle for "good enough" as you do this important work, look out for opportunities to gain feedback whenever you can. Seek out the improvement-minded people who will notice you for what you are doing, hopefully offering some well-earned encouragement such as, "You're on the right track, keep working at it."

"Love and work" is what people need for happiness, according to Freud. Both of these are core to nurturing your intrinsic motivation, as they are all about connecting. Love connects you to other cherished individuals, while through work you connect with others and the world beyond. And, of course, using your 3G Mindset to actually love work is an ideal outcome for you from this book.

PURPOSE

Set yourself a long-term goal with a compelling "why"—your highest personal reason you want to truly engage in improving your mindset—to inspire and direct you. Start out with an inspiring vision of where you want to end up, of who you would like to become. Imagine how your life will be different as you become that person. How will others react? What opportunities might it spawn?

Having that compelling why is like making a long-term commitment to yourself. Remember: making a long-term commitment before you begin can help you outperform those with short-term goals by 400 per cent.

More important, if you invest your energy in developing the skills to reach your goals, then your actions and feelings will be in harmony.

Instead of an erratic, disjointed onslaught of tasks, short-term projects will make sense as part of this larger context as you develop your inner *yu*. You can create a serene, underlying coherence to even the most chaotic day or week.

To go further, build on your inner drive to learn and create new things, to do better by yourself and for the world. And don't let a mundane job be your excuse for putting off what naturally motivates you. It's not about finding time outside work, but being creative about learning new things inside work, regardless of the job.

TRUE STORY—INTRINSIC MOTIVATION

Bo Hampsted is a long-haul independent truck driver, doing regular 3,000-mile-plus, coast-to-coast trips across the United States. When asked how he handles the potential monotony, Bo laughs, *"Bored? What, me? No way! You should see my rig. I've got a killer sound system inside, and before I leave, I pick a subject I know nothing about. I download and listen to the best lectures and lessons and, by the time I reach the other coast, I could pass the final exam!"*

That's why Bo Hampsted speaks four languages passably well, and knows more about US natural history than almost anyone around.

As you can see, like Bo, your intrinsic motivation can launch you on an exciting, challenging and engaging quest. It sets you up to begin the real work on optimizing your 3G Mindset, which starts now.

The Why Challenge

Great self-improvement begins with one word: "Why?" Why do you want to improve? Why change? Why would you go to the trouble and effort to learn new ways of thinking and behaving? Your why fuels your will.

And without will, you *won't*. But with an intense enough why, you can take on anything!

> ➤ He who has a why to live can bear almost any how.
>
> – *Friedrich Nietzsche*

If you've ever seen a single mother working hard in two thankless jobs to keep her children fed and sheltered, you've seen the intensity of why. If you've ever really sacrificed something big for something bigger, you know the intensity of why. And if you are ready to become someone who really makes a difference in your chosen vocation during your brief stint on this planet, then you *feel* the intensity of why.

Your brain, in fact your whole body, responds to *intensity*. Intensity fuels your body with oxygen, blood and a host of high-octane chemicals (microproteins called neuropeptides, hormones, etc.) that spur you into action. And your brain reflects intensity by literally lighting up in response. This is why intensity is one of the four clusters of grit. But intensity, and the intensity of your why can fuel *all* facets of your 3G Mindset. It can also fuel how quickly you improve your mindset.

Intensity Matters

Your intensity will therefore be powered by the degree to which you care about specific facets of your mindset and the potential role you perceive them playing in your prospects within and beyond work.

To help you intensify your why, we have listed here some of the factors that your 3G Mindset predicts and drives. These are the things you should see improved as your 3G Mindset gets stronger.

Here's the challenge: pick the three items from this entire list that are most important to you. Another way to think about it is that, as your 3G Mindset measurably improves, in what three specific ways do you most hope to benefit? Circle your top three choices now.

3G Mindset—Predictors and Drivers			
Accountability	Agility	Capacity	Contribution
Determination	Diet	Energy	Engagement at work
Exercise	Focus	Fortitude	Genetics
Happiness	Health	Improvement	Income
Innovation	Leadership	Learning	Longevity
Optimism	Pace	Parenting	Peace of mind
Performance	Perseverance	Persistence	Problem solving
Productivity	Promotion	Quality of life	Relationships
Reliability	Respect	Stress	Trust

Consider these your personal 3G drivers. These drive you to care, engage and improve.

CHAPTER RECAP

Reset your mindset with these scientific breakthroughs.

Myelin
The more focused and intense you are about a specific activity, thought or belief, the more myelin or coating you develop.

Deep Practice
Happens when you *intensely* focus on, struggle through, repeat and improve a specific behaviour, a defined pattern of thought or action.

Hard-wiring
Laying down a new improved pathway by forming deliberate shortcuts that lead to superior performance.

Neuroplasticity
The brain's capacity to reshape, reroute and rejuvenate as a result of experience. Ability to physically increase your brain's capacity.

Genetic Switches
The switches you have or don't have are determined by your parents. Which ones get turned up or down, on or off, can be largely influenced by you.

Epigenetics—Study of how gene behaviour changes.

G × E—Genes multiplied by environment.

People Make the Difference
You need others when forming specific facets of a 3G Mindset. And you are far more influenced by the people around you than you might realize.

Situational Forces
How you feel, what you do and your physical make-up right down to the chemistry in your brain is programmed to be directly influenced by others.

Science of Motivation
Three main drivers of motivation: (1) behavioural, (2) external and (3) intrinsic.

If we combine the main ideas of this chapter, we might say: "By now you are probably feeling intrinsically motivated to enjoy the rich sense of *yu* that comes from engaging in deep practice to harness your epigenetic powers and hard-wire (myelinate) an even better mindset, one G at a time." Okay, that's a mouthful.

Let's make it simple. The next three chapters will equip you with the tools you need to master your mindset, so you can apply yours at work and in life, beginning now.

GROW YOUR MINDSET: GLOBAL

Curiosity is one of the permanent and certain characteristics of a vigorous mind.

– Dr Samuel Johnson

The Global Clusters

Global:
The vantage point of your 3G Mindset. It is about openness to new experiences and new ideas as well as the ability to make new connections and to create new combinations.

Connectivity

Connected broad-minded
boundaryless big picture
relationship builder
collaborative contributor
wise Interdependent
environmentally aware
think beyond
streetwise

Openness

Open flexible
adaptable embracing
diverse curious
innovative multicultural
creative holistic
think differently
agile

Most people think "global" means being multiculturally aware or sensitive. When used authentically, this can be helpful. But, frankly, that version of global just isn't enough. When it comes to getting and keeping the best jobs, global, from the 3G perspective, is so much more.

THE REAL STORY— WHERE THAT OTHER "GLOBAL" CAN FALL SHORT

Vijay worked his way up to director of operations at his company's call centre in Bangalore, India, with more than two thousand people reporting to him. He prided himself on his "global mindset", having attended school in London, worked for a multinational company with headquarters in the United States and even hired people from diverse regions and backgrounds within India. He felt comfortable interacting with people from all over the world, watched cricket matches against teams from other continents, even ate international cuisine when "the big bosses" came to town, and really prided himself on being a global citizen.

His attention to detail, tracking how every call centre representative spent every second of every day (literally), helped him devise new ways to increase productivity. But, over time, as "handle time" (the time it takes to process a call) decreased and productivity (the number of calls answered in a given period of time) increased, customer service ratings began to plummet. So he worked his people harder, gave them motivational speeches, and offered small cash incentives for better results. Things only got worse. His regional vice president offered to help, and even suggested Vijay reach out to his colleagues at other call centres across the world to see if they had any ideas. Instead, Vijay stubbornly kept intensifying the formula he had learned in business school. Within a couple of months, he lost his job, mystified over how he could fall so fast from being the rising star.

Vijay may have had a multicultural mindset, but he lacked a true *Global* Mindset. Had he put on the 3G global lens and demonstrated the qualities you see listed at the front of this chapter—had he thought about his business objectives more holistically, been flexible and adaptable enough to reach beyond his immediate world, thought about the big picture, connected collaboratively with others and openly, curiously sought new ideas—his star would have shone bright. It takes the right kind of Global Mindset.

Specifically, Vijay could have done what you can do in any job to demonstrate and strengthen your Global Mindset. He could have asked questions rather than have made assumptions.

Some good Global Mindset questions include:

- "What are my blind spots?"
- "What assumptions might I be making that are preventing me from solving this problem in a better way?"
- "Whom can I reach out to beyond my immediate world to get some fresh ideas and perspective?"
- "If I think beyond our company or even our industry, who can potentially offer the best advice and share some global best practices for what I do?"
- "If I wanted to get two or three diverse perspectives on this situation, who else out there, beyond us, is best qualified to share some insights and advice?"
- "If we turn this problem upside down or inside out, how might we view it differently?"
- "What do those closest to the problem, including our customers, think the core issues are?"

Now that you understand and have measured your 3G Mindset, and you know the basic science of how 3G works, you are ready to strengthen and reap the benefits of your efforts. Since global is about the vantage point from which you stand and within which good and grit operate, it makes perfect sense to start strengthening your mindset with this first of the 3Gs: global.

There are countless ways to get global. The two main tools we provide you in this chapter—superconnecting and personal 3G GPS—are designed to (A) go beyond, even challenge the conventional wisdom to offer you something new, and (B) equip you to truly shine in any phase of your career. Again, our tools and the related tips are based on the combination of what the top employers say they value most and what the best science reveals to be most effective.

Growing a more Global Mindset can create immediate, ongoing and profound results regardless of your position at work, age or stage in life. It can change and enrich the way you see and approach everything and everyone.

You can begin immediately by doing a deep review of the list of Global Mindset qualities provided at the front of this chapter. Soak in each one, and let it penetrate beneath the surface. Pause between each. Having a Global Mindset is not achieved by saying to yourself, "Okay, I get it. I need to act more connected and more open." Nor is it achieved by employing quick-fix tips for appearing more global. You want these qualities to become infused as an authentic part of your lens through which you see and navigate every situation. Mindset is first about how you see, which then naturally affects what you do.

You can apply global anywhere. You will be pleased to know that you don't have to go on an amazing trip to a foreign land to radically alter your lens or the way you see the world. You can take an equally awakening journey within yourself. You can "go global" in the simplest ways.

THE REAL STORY—GO GLOBAL

When we were both attending a global gathering of leaders for the Young Presidents' Organization in Argentina, one of the features was side trips to the rural areas, ranging from Patagonia to the sea. Paul was travelling through one of the remote towns with the group in a small bus when suddenly the leader of the group shouted, "*¡Alto!* Stop, *por favor*. Please! Here!"

The group disembarked and the leader took them into what looked like a mechanic's garage. "This place makes the finest polo mallets in the world!" he declared. He then proceeded to show us around, giving us an overview of the materials, how the mallets are made, and why they are the very best.

Over in the corner, one of the group, Jeff, came in the back door and immediately sat down on one of the crates to take notes. He'd stop, stand up, disappear, take some photos and come back—writing and clicking, writing and clicking with this tremendous intensity. Back on the bus, Paul asked him if he would be willing to share what he was documenting. Jeff said, "You know what's amazing about this place? It's not what they make. It's what they throw out! Did you see the backyard? It's stacked with rejects. There are piles and piles of the mallets they don't keep. I bet they sell them to their competitors at a discount or sell them under a different brand. They only put their brand on the absolute best.

I'm a building contractor, and I suddenly realized we do the opposite. We take everything that comes our way. Some of the projects are downright ugly. The best you can do is put lipstick on the pig. And they are still pigs. But we put our name on all of them, good and bad. To be recognized as the best, you have to put your name only on the best! This is going to change the way we do business! I can't wait to get back and tell my team."

Like Jeff, you can learn to apply your Global Mindset. It's important to point out that if Jeff were applying for a job today, the same curiosity, connectivity, openness and lack of boundaries he showed by seeking ideas beyond his immediate horizons would be a huge advantage. Jeff could just as well be an entry-level supervisor who noticed, asked and sought an answer to something others did not. Think about the value his epiphany will bring to his employer. This is exactly the sort of thing employers we surveyed refer to when they say that, on average, one person with the right mindset is worth seven "normal" hires. We see no reason why that one person can't be you.

As acclaimed leadership strategist Dr Stephen Cohen says, you need to move beyond the old adage "'Think globally and act locally.' It is now 'Think and act both globally and locally' at the same time."

Jeff didn't need to actually travel to find that example or solution. He could have (A) gone online to do his research, or (B) asked his network of friends and colleagues for their best examples of the best. It's about the distance you travel in your mind, not in a plane. To succeed in today's complex world, your Global Mindset will become central to everything you do.

Microchallenge:
Global Mindset

To strengthen your Global Mindset, you can do what Jeff did by

1 Cranking up your curiosity, seeking new ways to make what you do and where you work even better.

2 Entering each situation with an open mind, being receptive to and agile in adjusting to new ways of doing things. Be one of the ones who asks, "Why not?" instead of "Why should we?"

3 Reaching beyond your immediate horizons to harvest fresh thinking and form new connections between people and situations that others might not spot.

4 Challenge yourself every time you go anywhere (a restaurant, a shop, walking through town, etc.) to find one example of something unrelated to your work that offers an inspiration or idea that could lead to any kind of improvement, big or small, at work.

And that's just a start. No matter how strong your Global Mindset may be, it can always be stronger. And the stronger it is, the more of an advantage you will have at work and beyond.

Microchallenge:
Global

Pause and answer these questions quickly, honestly and from the gut.

1 On a scale of 1 to 10, how networked and connected are you to the wider world?

A. _____

_____

2 On a scale of 1 to 10, how genuinely curious and open are you to what's new and different?

A. _____

_____

3 On a scale of 1 to 10, how wide is your horizon? Or do you tend to focus on your immediate world? (a 10 is completely global in perspective and context)

A. _____

_____

4

On a scale of 1 to 10, how often do you ask questions of people beyond your immediate reality and generate new ideas?

A._____

_____

5

On a scale of 1 to 10, to what extent do you understand, appreciate and consider how you and what you do fit into the big picture of the world and the global economy?

A._____

_____

Knowing the increasingly critical role global will play in your success, how happy are you with your scores on the microchallenge? Consider these as well as your 3G Panorama results to be your starting point. The tools you gain and begin to use in this chapter will help you boost each of the qualities that make up your Global Mindset, thereby increasing your chances of getting the job you want.

Global: Up-and-Comers, Builders, Finishers

These tools tend to play out differently depending on your Gen G stage, although, contrary to some stereotypes, there are people with high and low global scores within each of the three stages.

Many **up-and-comers** may naturally have a more Global Mindset and therefore score higher on global than do the builders and finishers.

If you're an up-and-comer, or possibly a builder, you may be surrounded by people who are tapped into the World Wide Web 24-7 through one or more mobile devices they use to connect with others constantly. If you are one of these people, it's nothing to you to watch a video from India, to see a friend's photos from Croatia or to connect with a charity in Africa, all while sipping a cup of coffee at a local café featuring free wireless music downloads from Brazil. The world is boundaryless. You know no different.

But that doesn't mean you take full advantage of what's at your fingertips at any moment. Our experience is that even the majority of the most privileged and "wired" college students under-optimize global. On this dimension of your 3G Mindset, almost all of us can be stronger and gain ground.

Builders score across the whole range, from low to high. Some score very high on global, demonstrating exceptional awareness of and sensitivity to both the lack of boundaries of the extended network, and the greater ripple effect of what one says and does may have on others. Some builders, on the other hand, score terribly low, showing no real sense of anything or anyone beyond their immediate sphere.

If you're a builder, you have probably been both an observer and a participant as the world turned global. You know that the game has changed, and you may be enjoying playing by the new rules. Our goal is to help you win at the new game, so you consistently come out on top. Understanding and truly *thinking* global are two different things.

Finishers often score lower on global than their counterparts from the other two groups. But not all do. Some are pioneers for their segment of Gen G, showing the rest of us what thinking global is *really* all about. They may not have the same gadget-obsessed connections as the up-and-comers, but they can bring global to life in other ways.

And because they are less swayed by fashion and trends, many finishers may simply be more gadget efficient, using one or two gadgets to do the essential tasks rather than the four or five many younger people sport wherever they go. Some finishers are global agnostic. They score low and simply don't care, because they fail to realize how much more momentum and strength they could finish their working lives with if they only added this G to their mindset.

Connectivity

The vast majority of people representing all three of the subgroups of Gen G have one thing in common. They can all benefit substantially by improving their Global Mindset. You can too. Connectivity—the first cluster composing your Global Mindset—is about more than merely harnessing the power of your networks. It is about that combined with having the big-picture perspective and a sense of interdependence and collaboration, being relationally minded and showing the wisdom to maximize the seen and unseen opportunities that arise. Your mindset *qualities* are what enable to you realize the full power of the *quantity* of connections you have at your disposal. How better to begin than by becoming a superconnector who taps the full power of eight thousand people's ideas, resources and potential help?

Become a Superconnector

"Networking" is one of those overused terms that can make anyone but the most extroverted glad-hander cringe. Given how often we see master networking skills backfire, we feel compelled to challenge the "network your way to success" career advice. Plus, is your success really determined by the size of or how hard you pump your contact list? Or does the quality of your network and how you use it matter more? You don't have to be a monster networker to become a *master* superconnector.

The tougher the job market gets, the more important the quality of your network—those people to whom you are connected—becomes. Despite the tremendously helpful surge in online job searches, employers have told us that in difficult times a larger and larger percentage of people get the *best* jobs through people they know, not through advertisements or generic job postings they answer. Read that twice because it can change your entire opportunity-building approach.

Yes, quality *does* matter. There's a difference between getting "a job" that just pays the bills and landing "*the* job", the one you really want. Who gets the best jobs in the worst of times? Again, your network can make all the difference. The good news is there is a wave of new, great, even breakthrough research on human networks, and how they work. The bad news is most of us are terrible at putting our networks to good use.

The number of people who actively use some form of social media, through the internet, continues to explode. These are used for personal and professional purposes, but with varying degrees of success. They can be the best and worst use of your precious time. Some people invest (waste?) tremendous amounts of time with their online "friends", but with little real benefit. Others have an array of rich connections and grow their best opportunities through these channels. We are huge advocates of social networking used in the *right* ways.

The research tells us that even those people who have big, extended networks tend actually to interact with the same small group on a regular basis. These people make up what Professor Robin Dunbar has described as our "grooming partners", the little subgroup we rely on for support when disputes break out. It's like having two hundred neighbours living in the apartment building next door, but only interacting with the same two to five on the ground floor. The image below depicts this.

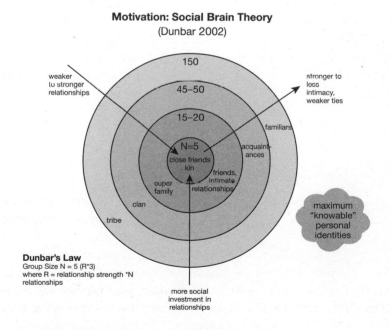

Motivation: Social Brain Theory
(Dunbar 2002)

weaker to stronger relationships

stronger to less intimacy, weaker ties

150

45–50

15–20

N=5
close friends
kin

familiars

acquaintances

friends, intimate relationships

super family

clan

tribe

maximum "knowable" personal identities

Dunbar's Law
Group Size N = 5 (R*3)
where R = relationship strength *N
relationships

more social investment in relationships

Superconnectors are people who grow an exceptionally high-quality network that extends way beyond the perceived boundaries and use it in an unusually effective way. You have to use your mindset qualities to move from networker to superconnector.

THE REAL STORY—SUPERCONNECTOR

Tom Schaff's job story is a great example of how global (mixed with some grit and good) can help you win.

Tom had just been promoted to become the youngest account executive at the well-known advertising agency Carmichael Lynch. Shortly after, the agency lost some business and he lost his job.

Tom knew that, in a tight economy, his best chance was to find a job doing something he loved more than anything else. He went through all his possessions and made a list of products and services he liked and companies he admired. His search included going through books and magazines, and wasn't finished until he had a hundred companies he thought he could passionately work for.

Tom's next step was even more novel. He printed out one hundred copies of his "companies I'd die to work for" list and began sharing it with *every* person he ran into. Seriously!

While walking down a Minneapolis street, he passed a person he hadn't seen in nine years, Brian Wilson. As a freshman at the University of North Dakota (UND), Tom was a student senator who voted to reduce Brian's student concert budget. The face was familiar, but they were hardly friends. But Tom needed a job and was committed. He turned around and was surprised to see that Brian had turned around too.

"Hey, are you Brian Wilson?"

"Yeah . . . Tom Schaff?"

"Yeah."

"Haven't seen you in years, what are you doing?"

"Just got laid off, fired. Looking for a job."

"What are you looking for?"

"Actually, I made a list of a hundred companies I'd love to work for. Care to take a look?"

Brian scanned the list and started laughing at the number seven company on the list, Creative Learning International. "How do you know about Creative Learning?"

"I love their Pocket Innovator and have used it for years."

"You bought one?"

"Yeah, why?"

"You're about the only one. They're small, and they're about to go bankrupt."

Tom proceeded to ask how Brian knew so much about the business and Brian explained that the company was started by Gerald Haman, another UND alumnus.

Brian offered to invite Tom to meet Gerald in two days at a holiday dinner hosted at his home. There, Tom employed his relational, collaborative, big-picture qualities to help Gerald think beyond the immediate possibilities. They quickly found out they had the same college adviser, shared fraternity friends and knew each other's relatives. Tom used his connectivity to create options when none existed, and he went into business with Gerald. He created an opportunity that previously did not exist.

Tom's advice: "Get clear on what you want, make your list, make it long and use your Global Mindset to share it with a hundred people. You have to be incredibly open, think way beyond your immediate world and connect. You can't use people. You have to collaborate and invent together. That's where most people blow it. They play by the standard rules. Let that list simmer and watch what happens over the next twenty years. It could take you places beyond your wildest imagination. Don't be surprised if searching for a job leads to the relationships that are most valuable to you later in life."

When you reread the list of Global Mindset qualities, you will notice that Tom demonstrated most, if not all, of them to achieve his goal. He didn't act as a networker shaking hands or using people. He was and is a superconnector, thinking big picture, exploring new ideas with curiosity and openness, even when walking down his local street. You will also notice his approach was intentionally low-tech, which proves high-tech is not the only way to connect effectively.

For most of us, our networks are under-utilized. It's as if we are using a Formula One racing car to fetch the morning paper. Even if you're not the networking type, you can reap the benefits as you look at each situation through a lens of openness, curiosity and connectivity to generate new opportunities beyond your immediate circle.

Our next story shows how another Tom did just this.

THE REAL STORY— CONNECTING THE 3G WAY

Tom was a reluctant networker. He didn't lack the skill set. He needed the right mindset. Tom had been a procurement manager for a large sporting-goods retailer for a number of years, but due to a change in the fortunes of the business in 2008, Tom was laid off. This change in circumstances hit Tom hard and he went to see an outplacement support consultant to help him deal with the transition from a steady job to an uncertain future.

Tom was surprised to find that the self-awareness-enhancing exercises that his consultant ran through with him sharpened his insights into what really motivated him at work, and he felt very energized by them.

He was also surprised to learn from his consultant that networking could open a lot of opportunities to him. Tom found this quite a difficult notion to understand because he wondered what on earth he had to offer anyone. His consultant challenged Tom's mindset. He urged him to be more open, to think differently and to think beyond his current reality. At first it was tough.

But as Tom began to recognize his particular strengths and talents and rebuild his self-confidence, he stretched himself. He decided to identify target individuals who might value these strengths and ultimately registered on one of the largest and most successful business networking sites.

Tom found that he enjoyed this safe foray into networking. He began to build his network by connecting with individuals with whom he felt he had something in common. He created a powerful profile, clearly setting out his aptitudes, strengths and career objectives, and quickly grew his network by joining a number of groups that reflected his interests. He also spent time participating in discussion forums and answering questions posted by others. He wanted to be sure to give at least as much as he received.

This activity got him noticed. Within two weeks of having joined the online networking service, he received an email from a recruiter who had been impressed by the obvious expertise inherent in the way he had answered a question on his page. Two weeks later, Tom was offered and accepted a role he now describes as ideal, which he believes would never have happened had it not been for the connectivity that the online network service provided. Tom had to put on a more global lens to see and tap opportunities that would not otherwise exist.

One common frustration people have with social networks—which can work to your advantage—is the feeling that people only contact them when they want something from them, just as Tom thought. Even if it is just the implied request to use your time to view their pictures and videos or read about their issues, they are asking something of you. The truth is people often use their networks for selfish reasons. We're all guilty of it. Think of the times you have reached out to someone you haven't had any contact with for a long time just to get something you need from him or her, even if it's an answer to a question or a piece of advice.

So start to strengthen your global lens by taking these two weaknesses—being near-sighted and selfish—and turn them to your immediate advantage as a practical tool, with three simple steps:

1. **Sign up.** Infuse your lens with curiosity, openness and lack of boundaries. If you have not already signed up for one or more social/professional network sites, do it. And try to sign up for those that are most recommended. Invite the people you admire most to connect with you and join your network. If possible, send a personal, non-generic invitation to them so they are more likely to accept.

2. **Contribute.** Give more than you get. Be an agile, collaborative relationship builder. Send a personal message to everyone in your network. Ask those in your network what you can do to help them. You may be surprised by how valuable others may find your connections and knowledge. On a regular basis (no more than once per week), send them *brief*, simple links, ideas, articles, quotes and thoughts tailored to their specific needs and interests.

3. **Extend.** Infuse diversity and thinking differently into your lens. Ask people in your network to recommend people in their own networks whom you should meet: others with whom you share interests or hobbies, their go-to person for various kinds of expertise and advice, friends they think you'd really hit it off with. Continue to grow your network by contributing to your core group and extending out into new paths.

THE REAL STORY—PURPOSE-DRIVEN NETWORKING SUPERCONNECTOR

Michael Kerrigan is a Washington, DC, lobbyist-turned-author and thought leader on issues regarding human character (www.characters-with-character.com). He's a master superconnector who is constantly expanding his network with exceptionally high quality people. How does he do it?

Authors do research, and researchers call a lot of people to get opinions and answers. Each time Michael calls, he says, "There's something I'd like to ask of you, but I refuse to do so without first making a meaningful contribution to you and the good work you're doing." He regularly refers to "the bank account" and his desire to deposit more goodwill and value into yours before he can accept any from you into his.

This has at least two positive effects. First, it allows Michael to build, maintain and connect with a high-quality network of individuals. Second, it makes those people more willing and likely to actively connect Michael with the other high-quality people in their networks. So Michael's simple approach has a multiplying effect in both quantity and quality, making him a true superconnector.

Microchallenge:
Superconnector

Being a superconnector is not just about growing new opportunities outside of work. The same principles apply to growing your visibility and opportunities within your current job. This enhances your chances of being retained, valued and advanced.

1

Whom can you reach out to and offer some value to today, outside of work, as a deposit on your network and connections of tomorrow?

A._____

_____

_____

_____

_____

2

Whom can you reach out to and offer some value to (ideas, help, time, resources, etc.) today to help him or her appreciate who you are and what you do tomorrow?

A._____

_____

_____

_____

_____

_____

Tap Your Eight Thousand

One of the best ways to strengthen your global lens and the opportunities you unearth is to tap into the power of what is known as "social network theory". Once you understand its message and potential, you will never look at your choice and quality of connections in quite the same way.

The big discovery is that we don't influence just the people we see and know. We can also have a significant influence on people they know, and even on the people those people know. According to Harvard and University of California scientists Nicholas Christakis and James Fowler and their Three Degrees of Influence Rule, you influence and are influenced by people three layers out in ways far more profound than you may imagine. But the only way to take full advantage of this power is to use your Global Mindset.

If you believe, as Michael Kerrigan does, that the more you give, the more you get, then you need to understand the full magnitude of what you now give and get, intentionally and unintentionally, through your social network. Once you understand this, you can then make much more intentional and effective use of your network to get the job-related opportunities you seek.

Christakis and Fowler are the gurus of social network theory. Through a groundbreaking analysis of data from 12,067 people, they discovered and proved the following:

> A person is about 15 per cent more likely to be happy if directly connected to another person (at one degree of separation) who is happy. The spread of happiness doesn't stop there. The happiness effect for people at two degrees of separation (the friend of the friend) is 10 per cent, and for people at three degrees of separation (the friend of a friend of a friend) it is about 6 per cent . . . And the amazing thing is that even people who are three degrees removed from you, whom you may have never met, can have a stronger impact on your personal happiness than a wad of hundreds in your pocket . . . We found that each happy friend a person has increases that person's probability of being happy by about 9 per cent. Each unhappy friend decreases it by 7 per cent.

In other words, mindset is contagious. This means you can use your mindset to positively affect others—their happiness, health and more—increasing the chances they will want to help you when the time comes.

The two main lessons from this research are (1) be more deliberate about surrounding yourself with people who enhance your mindset, and (2) like Michael Kerrigan, you can use your 3G Mindset to enhance your opportunities.

Tip: When it comes to superconnecting with your social network, focus on quality and let it drive your quantity, not the other way around.

The basic formula the social network theory folks suggest we adopt is this: 20 × 20 × 20 = 8,000. That means, if you know 20 people through work and life, and each of them on average knows 20 people, and each of their 20 connect with 20 more, then your mindset influences roughly 8,000 people, *8,000 lives*. For some, the true number is in the hundreds of thousands. It also means that you can potentially tap 8,000 resources to help you, since you spend some of your energy helping your 20. To do so, you have to think differently, think beyond, and think global.

Microchallenge:
The Eight Thousand

The eight thousand principle applies within and beyond your current job.

1

Take out a piece of paper and write down your twenty people. List those twenty (or more) people whom you know through work, clubs, community groups, teams, recreation, family, and so on. They don't have to be best friends, just people you know. Your list may be a dozen, or it could be in the hundreds.

A. _____

_____

_____

_____

_____

_____

_____

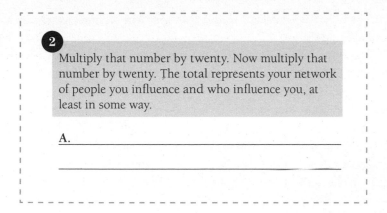

2 Multiply that number by twenty. Now multiply that number by twenty. The total represents your network of people you influence and who influence you, at least in some way.

A. _____

_____

Here's how it works. Let's say every week you send each of your twenty a note with a helpful, thoughtful link, idea, quote or suggestion. You make it routine, just like brushing your teeth or checking your email. And a few months later you need some help, say, coming up with ideas for places to apply for a job, or wondering whom to talk to about some career ideas.

You send a note with your humble request to your twenty, asking them for their ideas and if they wouldn't mind passing your note along to their network, so you can ask their twenty, and so on. You could even make it fun, offering a reward to the first one who sends in a great idea. By giving them a chance to do a small favour for you, you've done them a favour. You gave them a chance to reciprocate. Most will jump at the chance. When you employ this formula, everyone wins.

Note: 72 per cent of people say that charity/volunteer work has done more to expand their network of contacts to help their future working life than any other non-work activity. These people can later become a rich portion of your network of connections, which you can tap to help you expand your entire Global Mindset.

Openness

You can immediately use the first tools, superconnecting and tapping your eight thousand, to strengthen your global connectivity. Next, you can focus on building your global openness, the second cluster of your Global Mindset.

The openness cluster includes mindset qualities such as flexibility, adaptability, creativity, curiosity and innovativeness, some of which are in the top six qualities employers want most. You already know that the natural tendency is to limit your focus to who and what is immediately at hand.

Openness is about thinking beyond the here and now and being uncommonly receptive to diverse perspectives or ideas so you can tap a much richer array of opportunities in your career.

To do this, you must first turn on your personal 3G global positioning satellite, or GPS.

Turn on Your Personal 3G GPS

When you use a global positioning satellite device, one of the most amazing features is its ability to zoom in to incredible detail or zoom out to the stratosphere. This same principle applies to you and your Global Mindset. We call the different levels of detail in your personal 3G GPS "street view" (highly detailed), "sky view", and "space view" (zoomed out).

The busier you are, the more street view you may feel you need to have, considering only ideas or options that are within your immediate reach. This means you must be much more deliberate in your efforts to rise above or elevate to the big picture view to open your mind to new opportunities and ideas. It's amazing how, when you're lost or disoriented, seeing an aerial view can instantly give you the perspective you need to proceed with confidence.

As the world's top employers will tell you, it's extremely important to keep the big picture in mind and to be open to the wider consequences of our actions. Good intentions without a Global Mindset can lead to bad results. We want to help you get the best results.

THE REAL STORY—STREET VIEW

When hiking along a mountain stream that tumbled into the Sill River near Innsbruck, Austria, Paul ran across a group of teenagers from around Europe who had met up on their travels camping very close to the stream. He noticed they were tidying up their makeshift campsite and were using a portable toilet. As Paul paused to sip from his water bottle and chat with the group, he saw two boys go over to dump the portable toilet into the stream.

"Wait! Stop! Please, what are you doing?" Paul cried out. They paused, looked at him, kind of shocked by his concern. "Cleaning up everything, so we can pack up and hike up the trail," answered one of the hikers.

"But that's not good. That's not sanitary! Look, you will pollute the stream for everyone else!" Paul explained, as he pointed downstream.

Now more of the group looked up, caught up in the drama. "Hey, what's the big deal?" the boy holding one of the portable toilet handles asked. "Do not worry, my friend, we will not leave a mess."

In his mind, he was being responsible, considerate and clean. In Paul's mind, the group was being highly irresponsible, inconsiderate and foul. Had they had a personal 3G GPS, they would not have made such an unhygienic mistake.

Our discovery is that, especially at work, many people act like the boys dumping in the stream. They may have the best of intentions but they fail to consider their deeds and words in the big picture. It is astonishing how often people say or do something for an immediate "win" (laugh, pat on the back, avoiding a problem or confrontation) that really creates a larger loss (hurt feelings, delays, poor decisions, upset customers, and more). We see constant proof of how this can cripple one's ability to get, keep and advance within the best jobs.

That's why, for every situation, you want to consider using your personal

3G GPS to employ the three views: street, sky and space. When you do, it literally forces you to employ a more open Global Mindset, which allows you to see both impact and opportunities that you might otherwise miss.

The campers had only a street view. From their vantage point, they were using flowing water to create a clean campsite. Had they risen to sky view, they would have noticed that their stream flowed through several more campsites on its way to the Sill River, the main river through Innsbruck. And at space view, they would have realized that their filth would be flowing through an entire region inhabited by hundreds of thousands of people.

Imagine the same effect within a workplace. What you put in the river and whom it affects will be largely determined by how well you employ your Global Mindset and personal GPS.

THE REAL STORY—PERSONAL GPS AT WORK

Adam Eaton is the director of leadership development for Aviva, the fifth largest insurance company in the world. Given Aviva's aspirations when taking many different companies with different names and unifying them under "One Aviva", Adam brought roughly fifty leaders from various parts of the business to a special programme at INSEAD in France. It was a serious investment and a bold challenge.

At one stage in the programme, one of the leaders raised his hand and protested, "I do not understand why we are wasting our time on these Aviva issues, when we have more urgent issues, in our office, in our business, which need to be addressed now . . . Wouldn't it be a better investment to let us each work on our own immediate issues?"

The leader had a point. From a street view perspective, there were burning issues back home, in their parts of the business, that seemed far more pressing than Aviva's global agenda. Adam calmly listened, acknowledged the point and elevated the group to a sky and space view advantage. "You're right. There will always be those pressing issues in each of your parts of the business. But part of the reason we are here is to take a high-level view of the business. First, if we think about Aviva, we will never enjoy the advantages of being a unified brand and company if we do not get our leaders on the same page. Second, if we go even higher, we can see that if we do not achieve One Aviva, we cannot compete. This is about the long-term survival of our company, and creating a bright future together."

Time

Add time to the equation, and your perspective gets sharpened even more. Adam Eaton helped people think longer term. Likewise, if the campers had asked themselves, "What, if any, effect does this have right now?" the answer might have been "Not much." But if they had asked, "What, if any, effect does this have over time?" the answer changes dramatically, as their simple act contaminates far and wide.

Tip: Whenever you decide or do anything, pause long enough to ask yourself what are the potential far-reaching and long-term implications?

Global often prevents you from turning a local "right" into a much grander "wrong", which is very important. More than ever, the effects of our words and deeds flow into others' worlds. The context or vantage point from which you operate can make all the difference in how things turn out.

➡ **Global Tip:**
For every situation you confront, turn on your personal 3G GPS and click on three views: street, sky and space. Look at everyone else affected by your decision, your words and your actions, both immediately and far away, short and long term. Adjust your approach to make it as good as possible for everyone who is potentially affected or involved.

Employ Your Personal 3G GPS

Remember when you made a work-related mistake or things went wrong because—like the campers with the portable toilet or the leader in Adam Eaton's group—you were too limited or "street view" in your mindset. Or think about a work-related situation you are currently facing that you could handle even better using your personal 3G GPS. Then complete the microchallenge below by considering who is affected at each of the three levels: street, sky and space. Read through the campers example first, to give you some pointers.

Example—The Campers by the Austrian Stream (Campers' Perspective)		
Situation: We had to clean up our campsite and hike to the next one		
Response: We dumped and cleaned out our portable toilet in the stream		
Who would be affected by this response?		
	Short Term	**Long Term**
Street	Our group	People passing through The next campers
Sky	No one, really	Everyone downstream Hikers filling water bottles The stream's ecosystem
Space	No one, really	People drinking that water Everyone downstream The entire river basin and region

Note: In this real example, if the campers had used their personal 3G GPS, they probably never would have even considered dumping their waste into the stream. This tool can save you a lot of problems and help you be much more useful and effective in all you do, especially in the world of work, where everything you do has an effect on your future prospects and, potentially, those who influence them.

Microchallenge:
Personal 3G GPS

You can immediately apply your personal 3G GPS to any problem, issue or challenge in any job.

In the context of work, or looking for a job, what mistake have you made in the past or what situation do you currently face?

What is/was your response?

WHO WOULD BE AFFECTED BY THIS RESPONSE?

	Short Term	Long Term
Street		
Sky		
Space		

Finally, given the clarity of your personal 3G GPS, what could/should you do or have done differently to achieve a more positive short- and long-term result?

Imagine applying for a job and being the one who actually demonstrates GPS perspective on how that job or role fits in with the larger objectives of the business and the business's position in the marketplace. While doing so is clearly an advantage, if not a requirement, for top-level jobs, we believe it is even more impressive for lower-level jobs, when having a sky and space view of the business is even less expected. Infusing your personal 3G GPS into your ideas, input, decisions and actions at work will set you apart from those who are too buried in their immediate tasks to recognize the big-picture implications.

Personal 3G GPS Put to Work

David and Rena work for the same company—a big-name retailer—in the same office complex. Rena is a regional director with 742 people reporting to her. David just got a new entry-level job in the regional warehouse, as an inventory clerk.

Rena is under immense pressure from her bosses to "hit the numbers" by achieving their typically aggressive quarterly objectives. This can naturally shrink or dim her global lens by forcing her to focus on the here and now at the expense of the big picture. Stress has a way of doing that. But to be noticed and considered for future opportunities over many of her equally hardworking peers, Rena can turn on her personal 3G GPS.

David has a similar challenge. His entire day is consumed with the fast-paced processing of inventory changes and demands, as data regarding purchases and new orders flows in from around the region in real time. David's job is to make sure everything works perfectly and that his warehouse has exactly the right inventory at exactly the right time. But, like Rena, if David gets completely lost in the immediate, local and urgent needs, he may lose out on the opportunity to be noticed and considered for bigger things.

Both Rena and David can increase their chances of being noticed, valued and promoted over their competitors by going beyond street view and

1. Employing space view by asking and answering the question: "How do consumer and industry trends affect this decision (task, challenge, action)?"
2. Employing sky view by asking, "How does or could this decision affect the rest of the business? Are there any others making similar decisions in our business with whom I might collaborate or join forces for an even better approach?"

You can (and should) be asking the same questions in whatever job you consider or do, as a way to make better decisions, make fewer mistakes and enhance the speed and likelihood of moving up.

The personal 3G GPS is a tool we both use to influence every business and life decision we make. It helps us to achieve big gains and significant breakthroughs. And we're convinced that it consistently prevents us from making otherwise blind mistakes.

Openness, Innovation and Curiosity

Great solutions come from great questions. One of the things you can do now to immediately strengthen your mindset and become instantly more attractive to any employer is to tell less and ask more.

Employers love people who ask good questions, especially in interviews, meetings and the daily interactions at work. Why? Because it is the most obvious indicator of an open, curious mind. And you cannot innovate without first asking questions as basic as "What if . . . ?" Prove to your employer that you are not afraid to ask good questions, learn, challenge and grow. Even up-and-comers can lose this precious capacity.

James remembers hosting a seminar in central London that was attended by a number of very senior employers. They were discussing the journey that young graduates make from college to work and what might be done to improve the experience when one of the delegates said: "The problem is, students these days are taught how to pass exams. They are not taught how to think."

Whether she realized it or not, this frustrated employer had hit upon a theory that psychologist Liam Hudson had come up with in 1966.

He suggested that there are two methods of thinking: *convergent* thinking and *divergent* thinking.

Convergent thinking is when you use material from various sources and present it in such a way as to provide the correct answer. This is what students do. They gather information from textbooks, journals and articles and transfer it to exam papers in the way they have been taught. They gather and provide rote answers.

Divergent thinking, on the other hand, involves some more creativity. An individual would bring together a broad elaboration of ideas to find a solution when applying divergent thinking. Thinkers of this type tend to stretch the boundaries and let their imagination generate lots of possibilities. This might mean that you don't get the intended outcome, so this method of thinking is not generally taught at schools. But it can be extremely valuable in your career.

Microchallenge:
Divergent Thinking

People who think differently and ask good questions get noticed.

Whenever a problem or issue arises, be the one who asks:

1

What if . . . ?

2

Even if it can't be done, if it could, how would we do it?

3

If there were no constraints, how would the best minds solve this problem?

4

If this had to be solved in half the time, how would we do it?

5

Or, one of our client's favourites, ask, "What would Steve Jobs do?"

In chapter 9 we explain exactly how ideas contribute to how much value you deliver on the job. In the right situation, being the font of great ideas typically pays off handsomely.

One well-known method of developing divergent ideas is called "kaleidoscopic thinking". This is a term that Thomas Edison, possibly America's greatest inventor, created when he talked about how he turned a problem around to see it from every different angle.

Think about a kaleidoscope. When you look inside, you see a set of colourful fragments arranged to form a pattern. When you rotate the kaleidoscope, those same fragments rearrange to form a completely different pattern. This is what we and other employers encourage you to do when contemplating a problem or issue. Simply turn the issue on its head, make sure you are open to every option and let the ideas flood in.

Microchallenge:
Kaleidoscopic Thinking at Work

Take a problem that you currently face at work, perhaps one that you or others are really struggling to overcome, and ask your best questions, trying to apply some kaleidoscopic and divergent thinking to it. To help you come at it from a different angle and turn it on its head, employ your Global Mindset and ask these questions, which have been used in top companies worldwide:

1

How would someone who knows nothing about this problem or issue approach it?

A.

2

If we had to get this resolved in the next thirty
minutes, how would we do it?

A. _____

_____

_____

_____

3

If we could resolve one piece of this problem or
issue to create the biggest breakthrough, which
would it be?

A. _____

_____

_____

_____

4

What do we know to be impossible, which if it were
possible, would create an authentic breakthrough?

A. _____

_____

_____

_____

_____

5

How would the world's best problem solving attack this issue?

A. _____

_____

_____

_____

_____

6

What is the one obstacle that, if surmounted, would create the greatest momentum for us on this issue?

A. _____

_____

_____

_____

7

If we put absolutely no limitations on what's possible, what is the most outrageous solution to this problem?

A. _____

_____

_____

_____

These will help you suggest solutions that may sound far-fetched at first, but that might become more doable.

Your Global Mindset can be applied to those magic moments when you apply an existing solution to a new problem to come up with a better answer for all.

James's father, Sir Alec Reed, did this when he saw how he could apply some of his recruiting innovations to create order in the messy world of charitable donations.

THE REAL STORY—THE BIG GIVE

The original idea behind the Big Give was to build a website where prospective donors could browse through all the charitable projects and causes that are seeking their support and where charities could publicize their work to potential supporters. Thus thebiggive.org.uk was born.

Sir Alec Reed's idea was brilliantly simple and was derived directly from the concept of an online job site, only in this case the marketplace was not for recruiters and job seekers. It was for charities and donors. Four years after launch, the Big Give had raised £25 million for charities, including the WWF, Oxfam and Médecins Sans Frontières. Year after year the Big Give's holiday fund-raising campaign continues to beat all records.

This hugely successful idea originated from the model of a job site (a totally different industry from that of the charitable sector). Sir Alec asked, How can this be done better (cheaper, easier, faster)? A job site matches people with jobs, while the Big Give matches projects with donors. Had it not been for Sir Alec Reed's open Global Mindset, the Big Give would never have been born.

Encourage your natural curiosity, practise opening your mind, keep on working to find different routes through and you will discover that new, unexpected solutions will reveal themselves to you. Fostering your Global Mindset's wider perspective will lead you to the continual creative leaps forward that the modern workplace really requires.

Use your personal 3G GPS, become a superconnector and tap your eight thousand. This is how you strengthen your Global Mindset now and over the long term. This is how you stand out from the pack. And this is how you build your job-searching and job-enriching prospects for years to come.

 Global:
The vantage point of your 3G Mindset. It is about openness to new experiences and new ideas, as well as the ability to make new connections and to create new combinations.

CHAPTER RECAP

Global: Connectivity
Tip: When it comes to getting and keeping the best jobs, become a superconnector, using your Global Mindset to curiously, openly seek and build diverse collaborative relationships with people well beyond your immediate boundaries who help you think differently and offer a fresh perspective in all you do.

Superconnectors
They focus on forging high-quality connections to expand their opportunities.

Tap Your Eight Thousand
Make a list of twenty people whom you know and make a point of sending them interesting tidbits and offering them real value every week, which they can forward to their twenty contacts, and so on.

Global: Openness
Tip: To get and keep the best jobs, use "kaleidoscopic thinking" to view things from fresh perspectives. And demonstrate your

personal 3G GPS by showing you understand the job and requirements from street, sky and space view perspectives. It will set you apart.

Personal 3G GPS

This tool helps you employ street, sky and space views to every decision you make and do, so you make fewer mistakes and deliver far greater value at work.

- -

These tools will help you strengthen your Global Mindset, which gives you an immediate advantage in getting, keeping and flourishing in the job you want, regardless of your position or stage of life. As you combine your Global Mindset with the tools for good and grit over the next couple of chapters, you will quickly discover how powerfully and naturally these build on one another in all that you do.

GROW YOUR MINDSET: GOOD

Being good is good business . . . If you do things well, do them better. Be daring, be first, be different, be just.

– *Anita Roddick, founder of The Body Shop*

The Clusters of Good

Good
The bedrock of your 3G Mindset. It is about seeing and approaching the world in a way that truly benefits those around you.

Integrity

Honest loyal
trustworthy **ethical**
moral dependable
authentic temperate
genuine **solid**
balanced
sincere

Kindness

Kindness fairness
compassion **empathy**
respect humility
generosity value driven
earnest thoughtful
value builder
unbiased

Employers emphatically seek good people with Good Mindsets. The top six and top twenty mindset qualities that employers seek include more good than anything else. Other research builds the case for why these qualities are so vital to how likely you are to get, keep, advance and flourish within the best jobs. And if you currently are or aspire to be a leader, you can't shine without a serious dose of good.

Professors Michael Brown and Linda Trevino discovered in their groundbreaking research that the presence or absence of many of the same good qualities you see listed at the front of this chapter have a profound ripple effect on those around you as well as on how much value you are likely to bring to the job. Leaders in particular who demonstrate these qualities are far more likely to earn the genuine commitment, positive values (trust, honesty, fairness, ethics, etc.) and superior engagement of their people. Good creates good.

We have every reason to believe, based on our work and research, that this applies to anyone at any level. Good applies to you regardless of your status or position. Good is not a "nice to have". It is a "must have" if you truly seek to secure and make your mark in the job you love. It is a practical and essential lens and tool for achieving the sort of working life you desire. No matter how strong you are on global and grit, you simply cannot get there and stay there without good.

Why "Good" Isn't Good Enough

We cringe when employers tell us "We seek good people," because we know from our research and experience that they are asking for trouble. Some of the most miserable workers at any level we've ever met are good people who demonstrate good qualities. Some of the most pathetically performing and endangered divisions of businesses we've ever seen are filled with good people who are trusting, caring, ethical, and more. That's why books and thought leaders professing virtue and morality are at least partially missing the mark. Being a good person isn't enough.

The fact is, many if not most business cultures feast on good the way vultures rip apart the soft exposed flesh of carrion. The purest good lens can be shattered the first time it is pelted with reality. The work world is tough, complex and uncertain. If you have worked more than one day you know that to be true. That's where the 3G Mindset comes into play and comes together. It is only when you infuse your good lens with the strength of grit and the perspective of global that it can truly shine and endure.

So when we refer to "good" in this chapter and beyond, we are not referring to the common variety of being a good person who is so easily and tragically crushed. We are talking about the 3G version, who stands up to and is strengthened by the most difficult tests. This is the version that earns you the job you love and helps you flourish throughout your career.

And good applies to every aspect of your career. We are excited for you because world events can, and have, transformed the business importance of good. Continued crises in politics, finance and business have brought good back into sharp focus. It seems the worse things become, the more good matters.

For example, the global recession of 2007–11 created an implosion of consumer trust across several major sectors. This created what analysts refer to as "a flight to quality", meaning that consumers turn to those companies that stand by their values and don't lie, cheat or turn heartless to their people and customers when times are tough.

Here's why developing a Good Mindset matters and is so keenly valued. For any organization, none of these strengths can exist culturally if they are not demonstrated individually. In short, they must have (find, retain, promote) the people who stand true to what matters most, no matter what, the 3G way.

Good in Business

When trust in a brand's promise breaks down, the company that owns that brand can see millions wiped off its balance sheet in days. The best business leaders understand that they cannot sustain good profits without good people.

For example, Toyota, the global car manufacturer and former icon of quality, saw sales across the world slump after problems with both braking and accelerator pedals on their cars hit the headlines. When such vital safety concerns did not seem to be taken sufficiently seriously by the company, many customers completely lost trust in the brand and its promise, and thousands switched to other manufacturers. Not only did Toyota have to recall more than 8.5 million cars, its CEO had to emerge from the shadows to publicly apologize and pledge to rebuild the highest possible quality standards before these consumers would even consider buying from them again.

The fact that more than 50 per cent of the population actively factors ethical and environmental matters into their purchasing decisions these days only adds to the pressure for organizations and their employees to deliver at every level, everywhere. Simply to survive in today's marketplace, organizations and their employees must prove they are good, and live by the values they put on the masthead every day. The point is, you can use your 3G Mindset to prove to your prospective and current employer that you are the kind of person who will help them avoid such disasters and do what's right, especially in the moments of truth.

Paul Milliken, a VP at Shell (one of the biggest oil companies in the world, with more than a hundred thousand people working in more than 140 countries and territories), explained why Good Mindset qualities are some of the most important of all to him. "We have a set of values in Shell: honesty and respect for others and integrity," he explained. To Milliken, these are not theoretic constructs but necessities, no matter how pressurized the economic and commercial context he works in becomes. As he put it, in his characteristically direct way: "This is a long-term business, and you need to be honest and trustworthy or it will kill you." Finding people with a Good Mindset is a business imperative.

When Mike Mossman was vice president of customer service at DIRECTV, the largest satellite entertainment company in North America, he was responsible for the thousands of call centre representatives who were handling millions of customer complaints and demands every day. Their chief rivals were waging a brutal battle and seemed willing to say or promise anything to steal business away from DIRECTV, putting tremendous pressure on Mike's folks to do the same.

Despite the competitive pressures to make his numbers, Mike chose to take the high road. He told his leaders and his people, "We're not going to lie to our customers. That's not who we are, or what we stand for. We're going to treat them right, show our genuine concern and do everything we can to make them happy. In that way, we will earn their trust, and earn their business." You could feel the morale in the room rise. And Mike could soon see his employee engagement scores, employee retention levels and customer service ratings reach record levels. Good pays. And you can bet Mike Mossman puts a premium on good in everyone he hires or, as he says, "It's what makes the biggest difference. If you apply for a job with me, you have to prove you've got a Good Mindset."

Barry Hoffman, UK HR director at global technology giant Computacenter, told us just how important a Good Mindset is when it comes to deciding whom to retain:

> This is a pacey organization and we need people with the right mindset and approach. We are results oriented and people who are rigidly process driven will struggle. We are customer centred and focused, we want integrity and honesty from our people, so if you rally against that, even with the best intentions, it doesn't fit well in this company.

Again, to those who hire you and influence your future, a Good Mindset is a hardheaded necessity. Tom Peters, the world-renowned business guru, suggests that "good business is built on great people, decency, thoughtfulness and attentive listening". He has researched many historical stories and events and come to the conclusion that *there is an undeniable link between small courtesies and earth-shattering events.*

Tom Peters wrote, "The novelist Henry James said: 'Three things in human life are important. The first is to be kind. The second is to be kind. And the third is to be kind.' My observation: Kind works! And pays off!"

Peters then created a self-explanatory formula, which we could all benefit from maintaining in our minds:

Kindness (K) = Repeat Business (R) = Profit (P)

Tom Peters and these top employers are right. As you will recall, our studies with the 3G Panorama prove good guys *don't* finish last. They come out ahead. Remember: the 3G Panorama, including the good dimension by itself, predicts how much money you make, as well as how much value you deliver and, according to top employers, how likely you are to be retained.

If you have any doubts about the importance of good, consider what can happen when good is missing.

Paul recalls a global business leader—we will call him "Frank"—a billionaire who had made and lost his fortune more than once. He was using his tremendous grit (scored top 1 per cent) to pioneer an entire new industry across Europe. In the face of immense odds (regulations, public and political opposition, well-heeled competition) he was succeeding, or so it appeared. He had used his exceptional Global Mindset to think differently, reach out way beyond his immediate horizons to put together an international team and board and create a game-changing innovation in his industry. And nothing got in his way. He had it all. All, that is, except good.

Frank was beyond a doubt the meanest, most vicious, manipulative, selfish and amoral business leader we had met. He was essentially willing to burn and pillage his way through any situation and create complete emotional carnage in his wake. As a result, the immensely talented people who worked for him all quit, despite their large compensation packages, because the emotional toll was simply unbearable. And the only ones who survived were just like him.

It was only a matter of time before Frank's business crumbled under the weight of lawsuits stemming from their stream of lies and shady deals and the immense expense of trying to fill in the ranks with people willing to put up with a leader bursting with the inspiring power of grit and global but lacking any visible signs of good.

No matter how strong you are on the other two Gs, you can't stand strong or long without your bedrock: good.

The powerful truth is, for Frank and for you, we now know mindset is a choice, not a birthmark. A Good Mindset is accessible to anyone at any stage of Gen G. You just have to want it. And, at the risk of sounding like a sports shoe label, when it comes to your good lens, you just have to wear it and do it.

Good: Up-and-Comers, Builders, Finishers

Regardless of whether you are an up-and-comer, a builder, or a finisher, good applies with equal importance and power. However, how you think about and put good to use may vary.

If you are an **up-and-comer**, you should aim to ingrain the Good Mindset qualities into your lens at this early stage of your working life. The more you infuse and demonstrate the qualities contained in these two clusters of good, the more they will become second nature and require no effort. If you do not ingrain good early, your advancement and prospects will be naturally limited. If you do, you will be noticed. It's tragic when we see builders who spend years trying to gain back the momentum and opportunities they lost when, in their earlier years, for whatever reason, they failed on good.

A good mindset is particularly contagious. You may recall from Michael Brown's research that good induces those around you to be more committed, engaged and good. And it works both ways. You can deliberately strengthen yours by being around others who wear this lens. It's best if, as an up-and-comer, you can seek and find environments where good is appreciated and nurtured, where it is a natural, not an aberrant act.

As you apply for roles and embark on your career, make an effort to learn about and link to your prospective employers' values. Do this even before you speak to them for the first time. Strengthen your Good Mindset by seeking those opportunities, leaders and mentors who use good to achieve results, so these qualities are nurtured and strengthened within you. In particular, look for those times when you can go beyond being a good person by demonstrating your Good Mindset in the toughest moments.

If you are a **builder**, you have, most likely, experienced those painful moments when good backfires in an organizational setting, when you have to pay a difficult price for doing what's right. This may have jaded or bruised you enough to downplay and therefore under-utilize your good instincts. Or perhaps it galvanized your will. The important thing is to have enough grit to remain good.

If you are a builder, you will also recognize how truly challenging it is sometimes to really think and *be* good in the messy world of work. You've seen how telling a little white lie or bending the truth might get you out of a sticky situation, short term. But part of a Global and Good Mindset is to think long term and to strengthen your Good Mindset by not necessarily taking an easy but compromised route. You can no doubt imagine and likely have witnessed first-hand the beneficial long-term consequences that will come with being the one who is consistently dependable, respectful, fair and ethical. Your power comes from applying good not when it is easy, but when it is particularly tough, or when there is the most at stake.

If you are in the **finisher** stage of Gen G, good plays a potentially rich role in your legacy, the final chapter of your working life. And now is the time to bring good back to the forefront of your everyday efforts.

As a finisher, you may think you are about as good as you're going to get, for better or worse. You may be reasonably strong, and feel good enough. Or, like so many, you may have fallen into bad habits over the years seeing how others conduct business and have decided that if you can't fight them, join them.

Perhaps you've remained steadfast about good. Every great hero in every great story finds a way to demonstrate good in moments of real adversity. When you do, good will help you finish strong.

Professor Ronda Beaman is a huge proponent and exemplar of infusing authentic good in every interaction with others. But in her recent management communication course at the Graduate School of Business at California Polytechnic University in San Luis Obispo, she grew concerned that many of the lessons she had been teaching her students about focusing on others, generosity of spirit, expressing appreciation, demonstrating compassion, honesty, and more, were being supplanted by the "get ahead, do whatever it takes and take no prisoners" attitude.

Her students were texting, tweeting, pinging and zapping one another messages but had no idea how to express the qualities of good or to write a thank-you note. She feared that when it came to communication, good would soon be gone.

After some soul-searching, she refused to accept such a conclusion. Dr. Beaman realized a Good Mindset is timeless, but how you use it and communicate it changes. She realized, in her own words, that "technology may change, but approaching every situation and message with a Good Mindset is more important than ever. As efficiency grows, good becomes increasingly precious and you definitely have to creatively adapt how to help others put it to use." Good always matters, but how you communicate it and apply it may vary widely.

A Good Mindset is fundamental to building that kind of deep, sustained belief that motivates you and everyone to give their best. So how can you effectively strengthen your Good Mindset to encapsulate all of these qualities that employers hold so dear?

The Good-Strengtheners

We encourage you to engage wholeheartedly in each of the following three good-strengtheners—Impact Map, Personal Ledger and MyCode—with deep practice. Done right, they can build on one another in a way that they ultimately combine to help you truly master good in all that you do. And we have learned that each one of these tools has the authentic potential to be utterly game changing for you, both within and beyond work.

The first two tools will, with increasing levels of detail and intensity, help you see exactly how good your impact with and resulting value to others may be, so you can make immediate improvements. You can apply these to how you think about and present yourself for any new opportunity.

Seeing your mindset and improving your mindset tend to go hand in hand, especially when it comes to good. The third tool goes beyond impact and value. It helps you create the powerful shift brought about by actually employing the best aspects of your Good Mindset in any circumstance. This will make you measurably more memorable and attractive to any employer.

You need intensity and focus to make this stick. Simply scanning through these tools is like working the treadmill on the lowest setting. You don't benefit nearly as much on that low setting as when you show up to dig deep, dig in and really sweat.

IMPACT MAP

One of the most important concerns and questions any employer has about you is, how do you affect other people? The Impact Map provides clarity on where you are and is a simple tool to use to make your answer to that question ever more positive and compelling.

Earlier, when we worked through global, we revealed some of the amazing discoveries about how your mindset can impact so many others. These revelations tend to spark questions such as:

- Intentionally or unintentionally, whom do I most affect?
- How many people does or might my mindset really affect, and in what ways?
- In what ways do I, or might I, positively (or negatively) affect others?

A great way to come to grips with these questions is to complete your own personal Impact Map. Now that you are armed with the discoveries from social network theory and the three layers of impact you have and others have on you, we view the Impact Map as the next level, good-infused version of your personal 3G GPS introduced in the last chapter. Think of it as your pebble tossed into a pond, with waves that ripple out from the epicentre: *you*.

In this case, three waves will define your Impact Map. These waves represent the impact that you have on the people around you. The Impact Map combines effect and intention. Since your mindset is the lens through which you see and navigate work and life, the Impact Map reflects where, how and the degree to which your combined thoughts and deeds affect others.

For instance, taking your assistant out to lunch is a nice, considerate gesture. If it arises from genuine empathy, gratitude and generosity, you would score it maybe a 6 out of 10 on good, based on your pure intentions with a modest act. But if your intentions were political and inauthentic—buying lunch to squeeze more work out of your assistant or impress your boss—then it might score more as a 2 or 3. It's a nice gesture motivated by selfish gain, which generates some goodwill. If you meant to remember your dad's birthday because you love him with all your heart, but forget completely on his special day, it still might score a −6, given how much it mattered to him. If you had intentionally blown off your dad, it might be a −8.

You can see that doing this exercise requires complete self-honesty. That's tough. If you are unsure of your answers, ask those around you for their perspective. It's amazing how profound, humbling and, we hope, inspiring this single tool can be.

The three waves in your Impact Map represent near, mid-range and far, as detailed below:

Near—Those people in my immediate circle, most obviously affected by how much and what facets of good I have in my 3G Mindset and which I demonstrate when I am with them.

Mid-range—Those people in the next level, beyond my immediate circle, who are predictably affected in some ways by how much good I have in my 3G Mindset.

Far—The complete view of everyone who could even potentially be affected in any way by the strength of good in my 3G Mindset.

You can see a partial sample of an Impact Map below:

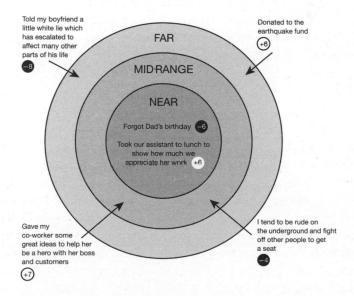

Microchallenge:
Impact Map

Now it's your turn.

1

Take out a blank sheet of paper and draw or, if you prefer, picture your answers to this exercise vividly in your own mind.

2

Draw three concentric rings or circles like the ones in the previous diagram. Label them "near", "mid-range" and "far".

3

Within each ring, and looking exclusively through the lens of the Good Mindset qualities, describe the immediate (near), mid-range and farthest (far) impact you have both within and beyond work (see example above). If you are unsure, ask those around you for their insights and verification.

4

To make it real, try to come up with three to five strong entries for each ring. Do your best to write down actual names of individuals or the names of groups whom you affect (in good or bad ways) through your Good Mindset qualities.

5

To add both rigour and insight to this exercise, at each level and for each person or group you impact, add your impact score, from −10 (extremely negative) to 10 (extremely positive). Factor into your score your authentic intentions and the effect you created.

6

Next, do an estimated average impact score for each ring: near, mid-range and far. Finally, average your average of those three scores. What's your overall impact score?

QUESTIONS:

How satisfied are you with the quantity of people you affect at each level?

A. _____

_____

_____

_____

_____

Do you affect more at some levels than others?

A. _____

_____

_____

_____

How is your impact distributed? Do you have a more
general (far) impact? Or do you have a more up-close
(near) impact?

A. _____

_____

_____

_____

To what extent and in what ways did your intentions
affect your scores?

A. _____

_____

_____

_____

Looking at your individual and average scores, how
do you feel about the quality of your impact? To
what extent do you feel you are living up to your full
potential?

A. _____

_____

_____

_____

What would happen if you could significantly raise your impact scores?

A. _____

_____

_____

_____

_____

Our experience with this exercise is much like washing a caked-on dirty windshield: it takes two or three attempts to get it right. Each time you repeat the question, things become clearer and you come up with more answers until you feel you have done a fairly complete job. Often those you come up with last are among some of the most important.

The Impact Map provides you an initial close-up in a magnified mirror. It's not always completely flattering, but the insights can be tremendous. It gives you a clear view of the current and potential impact your Good Mindset—through combined intentions and deeds—may have. Apply this tool throughout your day in all that you do. Aspire to earn the best possible version so, when employers ask, "What impact do you have on others?", the answer is one that makes you shine.

This next tool will help you fortify your case with any employer by taking a much more detailed, cold, hard look at the overall effect you have on the people around you.

YOUR PERSONAL LEDGER

Beyond the broad strokes of your Impact Map, in what precise facets of good do you contribute the most positively? These specifics are what will infuse and strengthen your CV, interviews and daily behaviour. In chapter 8, we'll show you how to use these tools and answers to at least triple your chances of getting the best job.

In what facets do you perhaps unintentionally create some downside? If you had to provide evidence, and you were to score 1 to 10 the magnitude of that plus or minus (10 is extremely strong, 1 is very weak), what would you insert in your Personal Ledger?

Accountants use ledgers to get a clear view of how the positives or assets (what you have) stack up against the negatives or liabilities (what you owe). Of course, you hope your calculations lead to a strong net positive. Now is your chance to apply some of the same objective discipline to your own mindset, behaviour and effect, by completing your own Personal Ledger. We find this activity tremendously illuminating and helpful. We trust you will too.

If you are currently employed, you will want to complete this tool in the context of your job. If you are looking for a job, then complete your Personal Ledger in the context of the people you currently encounter. We've added some of the ingredients of good along the side of the Personal Ledger only to assist you, not to limit your thoughts. You may wish to add others that you feel describe your positives and negatives more precisely.

Microchallenge:
Create Your Personal Ledger

Look at our example to envision how your Personal Ledger might look.

For this exercise, it is essential that you look deep inside your online 3G Panorama feedback (if you have it) or even your 3G Preview results, and yourself. You have to be brutally honest. You have to write down what is real and what is true, not what you wish were true.

1

For each Good Mindset quality either highlighted in your 3G Panorama/Preview feedback, or one of particular importance to you, write down a specific example of how you may positively or negatively affect others.

2

As you did with your Impact Map, for each example insert your impact score, from −10 to 10, to reflect the magnitude of the positive or negative affect you have on others.

3

Add your total positives. Add your total minuses. Subtract your total minuses from your total positives to determine your overall good rating.

4

Ask yourself, "Specifically, what can I and am I most naturally motivated to do to reduce the negative and enhance the positive impact I have on others most significantly?"

5

Write down three specific actions you commit to take, based on your answers to #4. An example is provided on the next page.

Example: Personal Ledger				
Personal Ledger	**Positives (+)**	**Score**	**Negatives (−)**	**Score**
Honest	I told my boss that I had slacked off and had someone help me to finish an important project.	6		
Dishonest			I called in sick just to avoid going to work, and my team was counting on me.	−5
Trustworthy	I let my assistant borrow my car to deliver some goods to a customer.	7		
Suspicious			I accused a co-worker of stealing another person's idea.	−8

Loyal	I didn't take up a recent offer to take a new position at a competing firm because I know I'm very happy here.	8	
Disloyal			I was really tempted to give my friend some confidential company information the other day so that she would score high on her college assignment.
			−4
Sincere	I sent some flowers to my colleague who had broken her leg over the weekend.	6	
Insincere			I purposely forgot to remind people of Joe's birthday because he's been a real jerk lately.
			−5

Example: Personal Ledger				
Personal Ledger	Positives (+)	Score	Negatives (−)	Score
Balanced	I took the time to listen to everyone's point of view in our team meeting. It meant it took longer, but we got a more rounded outcome.	7		
Unreasonable			I knew that my solution was the right one, so I pushed it through, paying no attention to my colleagues' views.	−2
Moral	I cancelled a major account and commission because a customer violated our values.	8		
Unethical			I lied on my CV, on two major items, to get this job.	−9

Fair	Tim gave the wrong information to one of our customers, but I gave him the chance to call them and correct his mistake.	8		
Unjust			Mandy was five minutes late for a meeting and I told her off in front of all her colleagues before finding out why.	−4
Total Positives: 50			Total Negatives: −37	
Grand Total (positives minus negatives): 13				

This example should have helped you to generate some ideas about what to put in your own Personal Ledger. Remember: you need to think about which facets of good you contribute the most positively to, and also those facets in which you perhaps unintentionally create some negativity.

Personal Ledger	Positives (+)	Score	Negatives (–)	Score
Honest				
Dishonest				
Trustworthy				
Suspicious				
Loyal				
Disloyal				
Sincere				
Insincere				
Balanced				
Unreasonable				
Moral				
Unethical				
Fair				
Unjust				
	Total Positives		Total Negatives	
Grand Total (positives minus negatives)				

You may have noticed that, for the sake of brevity, some of the qualities of good are not included in the exercise above. Do not let these limit you. If you would like to score yourself against any other Good Mindset qualities then, of course, you can. Refer to the list at the beginning of the chapter.

Everyone knows he or she should be good. And most of us know exactly what that means. As a boss, parent, co-worker or friend, we could teach others exactly how to be good. But knowing it and living a Good Mindset are two different things.

We have discovered that most often, when people fall short in making good a deep bedrock of their mindset, it is because they either make good superficial (deeds without good intentions) or forget or purposely ignore good, often in some critical moments, and sometimes for a long time.

Living the Good Mindset means consistently having your better self override your lesser self, especially in the moments of truth. One tool is scientifically proved to help you do this instantly and consistently. We call it MyCode, and it is a huge differentiator for standing out from the pack.

MYCODE—YOUR PERSONAL CODE OF CONDUCT

Imagine giving people an incentive to be dishonest, to behave unethically, with no apparent consequences. That's exactly what a group of researchers from three different universities (Duke in North Carolina, University of Toronto and University of California in San Diego) did when they essentially paid students to cheat in a test. The students could score their own tests and tell the teacher how many they got correct, and some would be paid for each correct answer. It was their decision. They could lie, with no chance of being caught, or they could mark the papers honestly.

Here's the twist: before the test, half the students were asked to write down the names of ten books they had read. The other half were asked to do their best to recall and write down the Ten Commandments. The idea was that, regardless of their religious beliefs or whether they even knew any of the Ten Commandments, just thinking about a moral code might affect their personal ethics. So what do you think happened?

The book list group gave in to temptation. They lied and cheated in an effort to get a reward. The Ten Commandments group did not. Simply by thinking about some kind of code of conduct before taking the test, they all behaved honestly, in spite of what they had to sacrifice to do so. Other similar studies showed the same result.

Exposing yourself to and being haunted by a code of conduct can have a profound and subconscious effect on your behaviour. It is a personal shortcut that makes it a whole lot easier to think good and be good. This same principle applies to the initial list of good qualities, the opening case for good and the good-strengthener tools in this chapter. By guiding you through a series of thoughts and exercises that bring the good qualities to the forefront of your mind, then having you apply them, you actually significantly increase your chances of becoming better and stronger at not just being a "good person" but consistently infusing these into your mindset lens.

The Ten Commandments study also, arguably, validates and vindicates the potential power of the corporate values statement, assuming three conditions: (1) the values are based in morality, (2) they are authentic and (3) they are used appropriately to elevate the behaviour of the workforce.

We believe this magical effect of "the code" can be made stronger by making it personal. Rather than reciting someone else's code, we believe you will get much greater value out of *your own* code of conduct. This challenge has proved to be one of the most profound and powerful for countless people who have completed Paul's programmes over the years.

Likewise, a study by Joseph Henrich at the University of British Columbia showed that people from cultures that belonged to a world religion (with beliefs that extend to other people beyond their relatives and everyday contacts) demonstrated higher levels of fairness to others— including strangers—than those who did not. In other words, those who had a clear code of conduct demonstrated more good than the rest.

And, as you know, the 3Gs play well together. Henrich and his team also found a direct relationship between how global ("integrated") they had to be to secure their food and goods. The more global they were, the more good (fairness) they demonstrated.

The interesting extra finding in the Ten Commandments study was that in neither group did people cheat as much as they could. Some refused regardless of any incentive or rules.

One of the ways good is improved is by removing what we call "the good should". Whatever you do because you feel you *should* is never as strong as when it becomes "Given the choice, I *would*..." That's the shift your own code of conduct creates. Autonomy – thinking and acting freely – is a tremendous motivator. Apply it as you create your own code of conduct.

We call this tool MyCode, and it equips you with a shorthand approach for documenting and accessing your own code in the easiest possible way. Our advice to you is to take this challenge seriously, give it your *finest* effort, so you create a MyCode that sings to and elevates you.

It should be something you aspire to live by and that, by definition, makes you a better person. A good way to think about this is to think of a simple, clear, memorable code of conduct you would give to your own children to help them to be better people, the kind others would seek out as friends and colleagues, and the kind employers would love to hire and keep.

Microchallenge:
Create a MyCode

1
Review your 3G Panorama feedback related to all the facets of good.

2
Note which good qualities were relatively low and which were most important to you.

3
Revisit the three to five good qualities you selected to improve in chapter 3, those that would offer you the most significant rewards when strengthened.

4
Write a single, clear, elevating statement for each one.

Sample MyCode

These are the principles I commit to live by

✓ **Elevate Others:**
I treat everyone with dignity and respect (even if I dislike them).

✓ **You Before Me:**
I concern myself with helping others before I help myself.

✓ **My Word is Gold:**
I am a person of my word, even when it's difficult.

✓ **Buck Stops Here:**
I take full responsibility for my words, actions and impact.

✓ **Go Beyond:**
I will consistently try to do more than is expected of me.

Creating a MyCode helps to effectively set out rules for your mindset, against which your behaviour should be judged by both you and others.

This example is not meant to be something you simply duplicate and say, "Close enough". Your code of conduct will be different. Yours will be *yours*.

Each time you pause, consider your response and improve it using MyCode, you are literally rewiring new pathways in your brain and lighting up new pixels for strengthening your mindset. Nothing can be simpler, faster or more powerful.

Hiring Bonus: In any job interview, you can highlight, share, or merely reference your MyCode as an explanation of your personal convictions and what makes you tick. Most employers respect and remember those who have this sort of clarity and proof. Use your MyCode to stand apart. In chapter 8, we will share some tips for putting your 3G Mindset at work examples into your CV, interviews and everyday working life.

So far we hope you have heightened your sense of importance for both global and good, and gained specific ways to help grow them, starting now. You have the vantage point and the bedrock. Next, you will need the fuel cell, the grit, to complete your 3G Mindset.

> **Good:**
> The bedrock of your 3G Mindset. It is about seeing and approaching the world in a way that truly benefits those around you.

- -

CHAPTER RECAP

The two clusters of good are integrity and kindness. Use these tools to improve both. Employers want not just "good people" but people who approach all they do with a Good Mindset, demonstrating these qualities especially in the moments of truth. Every employer wonders, "What effect does this person have on others?" These tools will help you define and strengthen your answer.

Impact Map:
A pictorial representation of the impact your intentions and deeds have on the people around you, whether near, mid-range or far.

Personal Ledger:
Your own "accounting" report to show which aspects of your Good Mindset create positive outcomes and which aspects unintentionally create negatives.

MyCode™:
Your unique code of conduct. A list of principles that you commit to live by and be judged against.

- -

Good clearly makes the difference. In the eyes of many top employers it scores at the top and utterly determines how much you are sought
out and valued.

A Good Mindset and a global outlook can help you shine, but without sufficient grit you'll have a hard time maintaining both, especially in
the challenging world of work. That's why grit is essential. It's the fuel
cell that propels you forward and ignites opportunities on even the darkest of days.

GROW YOUR MINDSET: GRIT

Understand
3G Mindset
Apply   Gauge
Strengthen

Only a man who knows what it is like to be defeated can reach down to the bottom of his soul and come up with the extra ounce of power it takes to win when the match is even.

– *Muhammad Ali, three-time world heavyweight champion*

The Grit components

Grit:
The fuel cell of your 3G Mindset. It spurs you on when others give up and gives you the grip you need to forge ahead. Grit proves that anyone can come out on top.

Intensity
Committed
Focused
Disciplined
Passionate
Purposeful
Energetic

Tenacity
Tenacious
Persistent
Relentless
Assertive
Determined
Resolute

Growth
Learning
Improving
Evolving
Striving
Engaged
Driven

Resilience
Resilient
Risk taker
Accountable
Brave
Courageous
Optimistic

As you have no doubt discovered, global and good can each be significantly life changing and job-prospect enriching. The third factor you can rewire and improve to enjoy immediate and ongoing tangible benefits is *grit*. This chapter will equip you with a series of tools to enhance your GRIT—growth, resilience, intensity and tenacity—which you can apply in any situation.

Grit is the fuel cell of your 3G Mindset. It spurs you on when others give up and gives you the grip you need to forge ahead. As with global and good, through our decades of working with people such as you all over the world, we have seen first-hand the immense and rich impact great grit can give in virtually all aspects of life. But it applies especially well in the job realm, equipping you to do what others fail to do to get and keep the best job. Grit is what allows you to shine when others fade and to stand strong when others falter.

Adversity plays a potent role in your career success. Most people who successfully land, keep and flourish within their jobs do so in the face of endless difficulties and challenges. At times, it may seem as if the challenges can be overwhelming and just keep piling up. Adversity and grit can play out differently for up-and-comers, builders and finishers.

Grit: Up-and-Comers, Builders, Finishers

If you are an **up-and-comer**, you may be no stranger to adversity. Entering the job market in the midst of or even on the heels of the global financial crisis can be overwhelming. This can either slowly crush or authentically fuel you, purely based on your grit. The worse the job market gets, the more grit you will need to set yourself apart by being the one who keeps plugging when others quit.

If you are a **builder**, you have, most likely, seen the wind taken out of the economy and job market. Chances are you have been affected either directly, by losing your job, or indirectly, by seeing others close to you lose theirs. It would be easy to succumb to the storm of uncertainty and adversity by feeding all your aspirations for a rewarding career into the shredder. Your grit will determine your capacity to gain that next opportunity, to sustain and fulfil your dreams.

If you are a **finisher**, you may feel a sense of learned helplessness, that nothing you do matters, given the severity of the adversity. Or you may feel as if "finishing" has become merely surviving. Our observation is, even in the worst of times, there is always that person who, through amazing grit, shines, who makes "it" happen in spite of all adversity. For you, that means using your grit to finish strong, even when the winds are blowing you back.

As you think about any job at any stage, it's important to realize that you are constructed for adversity. Much like the soldier hiding in the bush and springing into action at any given threat, our brains are poised, constantly scanning for and responding to any potential adversity. This is why, when watching the evening news, your brain responds with twice the intensity to bad news than to good news.

News channels know how to activate this mechanism. During an interview with a major TV news channel, the station manager showed Paul "the power provokers", the list of words the writers and reporters used to get most interest and the highest ratings. "Chaos", "catastrophe", "crisis", "tragedy", "situation", "battle", "war", "bloodshed", "threat", "terror" and "disaster" are among the classics. According to the host, we can now watch brain scans light up when presented with a "global crisis of unprecedented proportions", but hardly register an "emerging disagreement with considerable concerns". "Gradual climate variations" could never compete with "impending global climate disaster".

When confronted by a hailstorm of hassles at work, how you and your brain respond to adversity has become one of the most important factors in whether you are hired, retained or promoted. For many it is the most important factor. This is what grit is all about.

If you run a business, what would you care about more: how your employees respond to the customer when everything's fine, or how they respond when something goes wrong? As a leader, team member and colleague, what do others consider more valuable: how you react when everything's perfect, or how you react when things fall apart? Which one is more positive, has more potential, more opportunity to stand out in a good way?

And it's not just the big stuff. It turns out our brains respond differently to big adversities than they do to the daily annoyances. The big stuff can trigger one of the most powerful mechanisms in your body.

This is called the "fight–flight response." It unleashes some of the high-est-powered biochemistry you possess. Think of it as your own secret stash of rocket fuel. When it gets sparked, it can propel you to moments of greatness. We've all heard the legendary tales of the mother who lifts a car off her child, or the bone-weary soldier who under the enemy's bar-rage carries his fallen friend miles to get out of harm's way.

In organizational life, the big adversities might be a threat, an attack, a disastrous headline, the loss of a key leader, massive lay-offs, a strike or an unexpected change that throws all best-laid plans on their heads. The reality is that most people don't handle these sorts of things terribly well. But many do respond, shall we say, *intensely*, meaning they tend to react, and react strongly. The opportunity for you to be the one who keeps calm, focused and effective—responding with exceptional grit—in these moments is certainly powerful.

Less dramatic but equally powerful is the opportunity to be the one who responds to the day-to-day hassles, problems, annoyances and demands with uncommon grit. Like natural flaming-red hair, so rare is this quality that it can become your signature strength and key dif-ferentiator wherever you go. If you master it, grit could be the thing all future job references brag about when your name comes up for consid-eration. This day-to-day grit comes purely from your hard-wired pattern of response to adversity.

Microchallenge:
Grit

1

Think of the person you know who has the greatest grit. When the worst things happen, who responds the best?

A. _____

_____

2

What do you most admire about this person?

A. _____

_____

3

What advantages does he or she enjoy as a result of such grit?

A. _____

_____

4

What effect does this person's grit have on you, your trust and respect for that person?

A. _____

_____

As the creator of the Adversity Quotient theory and method, Paul has proven in his previous books and lifelong research that your AQ predicts and drives all facets of success. That is why AQ is the most widely adopted method in the world for measuring and strengthening human resilience, based on the 500,000 people who have measured and improved their AQs. That's why Harvard Business School has used it to equip today's and tomorrow's leaders. But grit goes beyond AQ, enhancing it with specific insights on focus, persistence/tenacity, growth and learning. This creates an even more robust and upgraded model for you to gauge and strengthen your grit, starting now.

When we ask top leaders to think of the employee who responds with the most exceptional grit, they usually get an odd, almost wistful look on their faces, then tell us *the* name. The point is, they *know*. More often than not, it was a past employee whom they hated to lose because he or she was so rare. Other times, it's someone currently on their team whom they clearly respect and value. When asked about that person's *real* value to the organization, the boss usually can't say enough about how great, how important, how valuable and how *rare* that person is. Here are the words of one global employer:

THE REAL STORY—GRIT

According to John Ainley, global HR director for Aviva, a FTSE 100 company, "I am lucky enough to have many examples in my career of the exceptionally gritty team member. They are rare but when you have one you definitely know it. The value they generate is usually a multiple of what most people deliver. A good person with grit is worth many who lack it.

"The one person who tops my grit list is Jon Hassall. He worked for me in three different jobs over my career in retailing and insurance. No matter what adversities come his way, he can get anything done. When other people make excuses, he makes progress. You just explain the problem and he is off to do it. He loves it when people tell him it cannot be done. That fires him up, and he always delivers, often in spite of the challenges he must surmount. People trust and admire grit, which may explain why Jon is great at relationships, has a wonderful sense of humour and achieves all goals with utter tenacity."

Notice his sentence "A good person with grit is worth many who lack it." One of our biggest goals is to help *you* be that person—the one, like Jon, whom an employer sees as worth his weight in gold. When you are, your job prospects will be forever enriched and your success will be dramatically strengthened.

Microchallenge:
Grit

1

Growth—On a scale of 1 to 10, how much do you really crave and seek ways to grow and improve, or do you bank on what you already know?

A. _____

_____

2

Resilience—On a scale of 1 to 10, how well do you stack up against the most resilient people around, those who truly and consistently shine in the toughest moments?

A. _____

_____

3

Intensity—On a scale of 1 to 10, how well do you maintain full energy and focus on the task at hand, or do you become distracted by other factors?

A. _____

_____

4

Tenacity—On a scale of 1 to 10, how well do you relentlessly stick to your goals, no matter how difficult they become?

A. _____

_____

Let's break grit down into its components and help you strengthen each. As you do, you will feel your grit fuel all facets of your mindset, helping you become more global and good even in the toughest circumstances. Your grit comprises growth, resilience, intensity and tenacity. Here are some tools and tips for each.

Growth

Growth is the view that, no matter how good or bad you are at something, you can learn and improve, at any age and at any stage.

Microchallenge:
Growth

1

Which relatively young person do you know who acts as if he or she knows all there is to know?

A. _____

_____

2

Which elderly person do you know who still has a thirst for learning and growing?

A. _____

_____

3

How does this aspect of the person's mindset affect your desire to be around him or her?

A. _____

_____

_____

_____

_____

Carol Dweck at Stanford University, whom we mentioned earlier, has created some breakthrough research with children that has changed the conversation about how parents raise their kids. One of the most powerful predictors of a child's performance and success is whether that child has a "fixed" or a "growth" mindset. If the child assigns his performance to something he perceives as fixed, such as intelligence or talent, he is less likely to try harder or improve, especially if he falls short. However, children who believe that effort leads to improvement and that one can always do better are far more likely to up their game. The same principle applies to us as we grow older.

We have noticed something distinctive about those with strong grit. They rarely, if ever, say, "Oh well, good enough," on anything of importance. They are far more likely to say, "That's really good. And we can do (or become) even better!" This improvement or Growth Mindset really sets you apart. If you constantly find even the smallest ways to grow while others stagnate, you soon gain tremendous ground, and may never look back.

GROWTH BUILDERS

One of the best ways to instil a Growth Mindset is simply to ask yourself at the end of each day, "In what way did I grow (improve, learn) today?"

You can challenge yourself similarly as you plan your work, "In what way do I intend to grow (learn, improve) by the end of this week? And what do I need to do to make sure that happens?"

We apply the same principle every time we get on a plane. As we each load our briefcases with the usual stuff (laptops, headphones, toiletries, reading material), we ask ourselves, "What do I want to learn during this flight?" Then we load the appropriate book, article or material to make it so. It's amazing how this simple exercise helps us avoid the brain candy (glossy, silly, tabloid-level publications) and stick to the more nutritious stuff.

You can make it more compelling by establishing a mystery, or question, such as: "What are the top five trends shaping my industry right now?" Or "What do experts suggest would be the best use of my commute time to work?"

Microchallenge:
Growth Builders

1

Ask yourself how you can optimize your commuting time to work or school.

A. _____

_____

_____

_____

_____

2

If you ride a bike, what can you think about or concentrate upon, or how can you change your route to challenge your brain? What can you spot and learn along the way?

A. _____

_____

_____

_____

_____

3

If you drive or take the train, what can you listen to, read, practise or do to learn and grow each time you go and come from work?

A. _____

_____

_____

_____

_____

4

On your way home and at the end of the day, ask yourself, "What's the most important thing I learned today?" It will help you store that lesson for the long term.

A. _____

_____

_____

_____

_____

THE REAL STORY—GROWTH BUILDER

When Paul arrived in Las Vegas to deliver a presentation, his client sent a driver, who introduced himself as Gil, to take him to the venue. As soon as Paul got into the car, he noticed a freeze-frame of a presenter on the video screen at the front of the car. "Hey, Gil, looks like you're staying entertained," Paul commented. "What movie are you watching?"

"Actually, that's my biopsych professor. I know it's a little weird, but I'm finally getting my college degree, online. That's one of the reasons I took this job. It gives me a lot of downtime in between rides. I download these lectures and zap back my questions and homework. It's pretty cool. And, believe it or not, it's a lot better than watching some stupid movie."

As the traffic got thicker and conversation continued, Paul discovered that in the past five years Gil had completed his real estate license and financial planning certification. He worked in that industry for long enough to pay for his biopsych degree so that he could pursue his real dream: to become a marketing consultant for big companies.

Gil woke up every day asking himself, "What can I learn today?" Or "How much can I cover between rides?" You can apply the same formula to any outing or vacation by simply asking, "What do I most want to learn by the end of this trip to help me be even more valuable in my job when I return?" Or "Of all the people I'm likely to be with in the next few hours, from whom can I learn the most? What would I like to be sure to learn from that person, before the evening is over?" We call these thought-stretching questions "optimizers" because they build you beyond the normal.

The same rule applies in any job. Ask yourself each day and each week, "What have I learned to make me better at what I do?" "What do I need to learn to grow in my role, or in this organization, and what's the best way to get it, regardless of what my organization does or does not provide?" Even in the most excruciatingly boring meeting, ask yourself, "What can I glean from this to help me grow or be better?" You may be surprised what you can find, even in the most morgue-like gatherings.

Beyond all doubt, those who have the greatest grit demonstrate the greatest growth. Make it your obsession. Let it be the worm that penetrates your brain and works its way into everything you think and do. That worm will keep you interested, interesting, valuable and improving—qualities any organization ultimately values.

The second facet of grit is resilience, or your capacity to respond constructively to adversity. Paul has found in his research that the most resilient people don't cope with or survive adversity. They *harness* it. And with our next tool, so can you.

Resilience

The work Paul has done for the past thirty years, related to resilience, with more than 500,000 people, has proved that you can both measure and *permanently* improve this vital facet of grit. Many of the key findings and methods are described at length in Paul's three Adversity Quotient (AQ)-related books. To help you build greater resilience, starting now, we picked one of our favourite tools for anyone seeking to improve his or her working life. It's called the CORE Questions.

RESILIENCE BUILDERS—CORE QUESTIONS

One of the simplest and most effective ways to think through and break through any barrier is to use the CORE Questions, which is a scientifically grounded tool we have used with hundreds of thousands of people worldwide. It is also a tool we both use in our personal and professional lives every time we face adversity!

The main rule is, there are no rules! The CORE Questions include four questions. You can use whichever one you think works best. There is no right or wrong answer. If one doesn't work well, try another. But use these four questions, and only these four questions, as they are worded. That's the discipline of the CORE Questions.

The CORE Questions

C—Control: What facets of the situation can I/you/we potentially influence?

O—Ownership: How can I/you/we step up to make the most immediate, positive difference?

R—Reach: What can I/you/we do to minimize the potential downside? Maximize the potential upside?

E—Endurance: What can I/you/we do to get past this as quickly as possible?

Let's take a sample scenario based on a real one Paul heard when he was in India, where people, many of whom may be competing for jobs like yours, sometimes show tremendous, even "over-the-top" ambition and resilience in achieving their goals. This tool can be used aggressively or subtly. No matter what your personal style, you can apply the CORE Questions to create breakthroughs like this one.

TRUE STORY—RESILIENCE BUILDER

Raj heard about a job he'd love to have. So he applied online. He got an autoreply. It said, "The application deadline for the position you have applied for has passed. Thank you for considering XYZ Corporation." So, clearly, he should give up. Right?

Or ask a CORE Question:

1. What facets of this situation can I potentially influence (to get this job)?

He thought about it and decided to call human resources at XYZ Corporation. He left a couple of voice messages and got no reply. Finally, on his fourth call, he got a cold, professional administrative assistant who said, "I'm sorry, but the application window for that position is now closed. Did you not receive the autoresponse informing you of the status?" Well, now, it's clearly over. At least he'd tried. Or is it? He tried another CORE Question:

2. How can I step up to make the most immediate positive difference (regarding this job position)?

So since the position was in sales, Raj decided to dig further. He called the receptionist and said in his most winning professional voice, "Good afternoon. I'm supposed to send a letter and some materials to the vice president of sales. Can you please tell me his or her proper name, title and address?" The receptionist refuses. He calls twice more, and the same voice answers. Well, he might as well quit. Or ask a CORE Question:

3. How can I get past this as quickly as possible?

He decided to call back during the lunch hour to see if a different person would answer. Sure enough! He asked again for the contact information for the VP of sales. This time he succeeded. Haunted by his CORE Question, he thought, ". . . as quickly as possible. Hm." So he immediately asked to be connected. Suddenly the phone rang, and a woman answered, "Ms Womack's office, Su-Lin speaking. How may I help you?"

Raj explained that he is the perfect candidate for this job, and he understood the formal application window is closed, but he would like to be considered anyway. Su-Lin politely listened, then said, "I appreciate your situation, but they are going to be going through the applications tomorrow, and Ms Womack is at a big sales expo at the Hilton downtown the rest of the day. But do feel free to keep an eye out for future postings." At least she was nice and let Raj down easy. You can't always get what you want and he'd given it a good try. Raj could walk away. Or he could ask any CORE Question, including:

4. What can I do to maximize the potential upside (of this setback)?

5. How can I step up to make the most immediate positive difference?

6. What facets of this situation can I potentially influence?

Almost any can work. Raj decided to go for it. He put on his winning interview outfit and drove downtown to the Hilton. It was a hassle, with no promise of bearing fruit, but he did it anyway. If you don't show up, you don't get to play.

Raj found the sales expo. He tried to enter, but they asked for his name badge. He was not on the registration list, so he couldn't get in. CORE Question:

7. How can I get past this as quickly as possible?

Raj grabbed some hotel stationery, wrote a note, and put it into an envelope. He wrote "Confidential" on the flap. He walked up to another door and said, "I have a very important message for Ms Womack with XYZ Corporation. Would you like to deliver it to her immediately, or would you prefer I just run in and hand it to her really quickly?" The usher looked at him, at the letter, and back at him. "I'd better take it," he said, and motioned to his colleague to cover the door while he was gone. It didn't go as planned, but Raj decided to stand his ground. He knew Ms Womack might be displeased, so he asked himself:

8. What can I do to minimize the potential downside?

Raj devised his plan. Several minutes later, Ms Womack walked up briskly and the original usher pointed to him. Raj's note had said that he had urgent information about the new sales position that he felt Ms Womack would want right away, instructing her to meet him at the door. "What's this all about?" she demanded.

Raj took a deep breath, reached out, shook her hand, introduced himself and explained, "Ms Womack, I hope you'll please forgive me for being so forward and so persistent, but may I assume those are qualities you seek in your sales team?" She looked slightly perturbed and said, "I'm sorry, this is no way to get an interview or win me over if that's what you're trying to do here . . ."

With a warm, understanding smile, Raj continued, "Please forgive me, but the reason this is urgent is because I want to be your next sales star, and I know from Su-Lin that you are looking through applications tomorrow. When I tried to apply and she told me the window was shut, I could have walked away; all five times I faced rejection just trying to apply. But I refused. I don't tend to give up when I believe I can offer some real value. And I know I can as part of your team. It wasn't easy to find you here and get you to talk to me. And I imagine your salespeople face the same challenges every day. You don't have to interview me now if you don't have time. If you do, I'd be delighted, of course, and will gladly wait until you have a few minutes for me to buy you a cold drink for us to chat. Either way, given what I've gone through just to shake your hand today, would you kindly at least consider my application? You'll see I have the right stuff to win the job."

Ms Womack paused, looked at Raj and his outstretched hand holding the envelope with his cover letter and CV and said with a small smile, "Well, you've got some nerve coming here and doing this . . . and, I have to admit, I kind of like that." Ms Womack paused again, thinking. "We typically abide by our deadlines on applications. And I'm going to be wrapped up in this expo for the next four hours. But I guess I can meet you for fifteen minutes at seven-thirty, before I head up for dinner, if you're willing to wait. I'll certainly understand if you prefer not to," she said, inviting Raj to walk away.

"Seven-thirty by the front desk. I'll be there fifteen minutes early in case you free up sooner. Thank you, Ms Womack, I appreciate your generosity and flexibility. See you then." Raj handed over his documents to review if she liked and promised to bring a fresh copy to the interview, just in case. Raj could see her shaking her head, almost admiringly, as she walked away. True grit (with a solid dose of good) wins the day.

Notice that Raj was respectful, understanding, empathic, warm and, yes, tenacious. This example may or may not fit you, your personality, your approach or your career aspirations. That's not the point. The lesson is that, when faced with a seemingly endless barrage of blockades, this person breaks through over and over again, using only one tool, the CORE Questions. And it takes a lot of grit to win what you want as you compete against the expanded pool of Gen G.

For what sort of challenges can *you* use the CORE Questions, and with whom? We hope your answers, like the hundreds of thousands worldwide who have put this simple tool to work, are *"for anything and with anyone"*. And you can pull out this tool to use immediately.

Microchallenge:
Resilience Builder

Employ the CORE Question tips:

1 Pick any challenge or obstacle.

2 Use the four questions separately.

3 Pick whichever one you think best fits the situation:

Which facets of the situation can I/you/we potentially influence?

How can I/you/we step up to make the most immediate, positive difference?

What can I/you/we do to minimize the potential downside? Maximize the potential upside?

What can I/you/we do to get past this as quickly as possible?

Use these questions exactly as worded.*

*This wording comes from decades of testing and honing. For more than twenty years, Paul and his team have been formally testing the effectiveness of the CORE Questions (and other tools) for measurably improving one's AQ and resilience. The initial tools were far more complex. But, over time, the resilience-building tools were repeatedly tested and refined. After twenty years, the CORE Questions are the simplest and one of the most effective resilience-building tools.

Intensity

Intensity is about focus with energy. It is something employers crave because the right brand of intensity through focus is almost a lost art. Our research indicates that intensity is one of the most difficult and vital facets of fulfilment and success.

Over the last few decades, diagnosed levels of ADHD (attention deficit/hyperactivity disorder) have tripled worldwide. Today people often use these terms as descriptions as much as diagnosed conditions, applying them to anyone who has trouble finishing a sentence or thought without flitting on to something else, which means most of us.

Just as technology tends to shrink our usable vocabulary, it also dwindles our ability to focus fully. Worldwide consumption of television is now over one trillion hours every year, while studies show that teenage vocabulary has dropped by half compared to the 1950s.

The internet and electronic media are beginning to take over from TV among young people, with a recent US study finding that eight- to eighteen-year-olds log an average daily exposure of just under *eleven hours* of electronic media.

Gary Small, a professor of psychiatry at UCLA and the director of its Memory and Ageing Centre, believes this multiple media use will have a profound physiological and neurological impact. "The current explosion of digital technology is not only changing the way we live and communicate but is rapidly and profoundly altering our brains," he says. He argues that the daily use of computers, smartphones, search engines and other such tools "stimulates brain cell alternation and neurotransmitter release, gradually strengthening new neural pathways in our brains while weakening old ones".

The problem is that stimulation does not necessarily lead to deeper intelligence. Author Nicholas Carr has been credited with asking if the internet is making us stupid. Carr cites dozens of studies from psychologists, neurobiologists, educators and web designers that point to the same conclusion: "When we go online," he says, "we enter an environment that promotes cursory reading, hurried and distracted thinking and superficial learning."

In most countries, research shows that people spend on average between nineteen and twenty-seven seconds looking at a page of internet information before moving on. While there's nothing wrong with skimming, Jordan Grafman, head of the cognitive neuroscience unit at the National Institute of Neurological Disorders and Stroke, points out how such constant shifting of your attention online inevitably affects your brain, making you "less deliberative . . . less able to think and reason out a problem".

And it's not just the internet. Texting and answering emails harms your IQ more than twice as much as smoking marijuana, according to a University of London study by psychologist Dr Glenn Wilson, funded by Hewlett-Packard. The constant disruption of "always on" technology means you lose concentration, leaving your mind fixed in an almost permanent state of readiness, rather than focusing on the task in hand, and at grave risk of what the study's authors call "informania".

So when was the last time you had an utterly uninterrupted conversation with someone, on track, in depth, with eye contact, free of all distractions? You see the challenge.

Microchallenge:
Informania

During your next break, focus for ten to fifteen minutes on one person or one thing. Close this book. Fend off all distractions and temptations to divert your focus.

What do you notice about the experience? What did you learn about yourself?

As the epidemic of what we have coined "focus deficit disorder" grows, the need to quiet our minds intensifies. Airport lounges now feature the sanctuary room, free of cell phones, conversation and noise so people can attempt to decompress enough to go back into their noisy world. Many trains feature a "quiet car", a low-volume travel option, for which there is high demand. Even personal technology is designed more and more with the personal sanctuary in mind. Portable devices offer video, audio and, increasingly, 3-D immersion experiences, all of which can be enjoyed with the latest generation of full-size, noise-cancellation headphones to silence the onslaught, if only for a brief respite. Many of the most expensive resorts find a digital-free zone to be a key selling point rather than a detraction.

Multitasking is a lie. Psychologist Dr Edward Hallowell (who is also a specialist in the treatment of ADHD) has even called it "a mythical activity in which people believe they can perform two or more tasks simultaneously". It turns out that what we think of as multitasking is really more like "multiswitching", as if you were watching multiple television screens. You can only really watch one; although you are aware of and can switch between the others, you are unlikely to really absorb or optimize any. The most dangerous and dramatic trend related to our inflated sense of multitasking is people texting while driving. Recent studies show that it is *worse* than driving while intoxicated. As much as we want to be multitasking masters, our brains are designed for the grit-enhancing quality, *focus*.

That is certainly what people believed in the past. "There is time enough for everything in the course of the day, if you do but one thing at once, but there is not time enough in the year, if you will do two things at a time," Lord Chesterfield wrote in one of his famous letters to his son written in the 1740s. What people today call multitasking, Chesterfield saw as the bad habits of immaturity. Instead, "This steady and undissipated attention to one object is a sure mark of a superior genius; as hurry, bustle and agitation are the never-failing symptoms of a weak and frivolous mind." The beliefs of breakthrough artists and thinkers agree. When asked about his particular genius, Isaac Newton replied that, if he had made any discoveries, it was "owing more to patient attention than to any other talent".

Nowadays, more and more research backs this view. Multitasking is actually about switching attention between different competing tasks, all the time judging which are the most important ones. Yet when a recent study by researchers at the University of California in Irvine monitored office staff, they found that workers took an average of *twenty-five minutes* to recover from interruptions such as answering emails or texts to return to their original task. Discussing multitasking with the *New York Times* in 2007, Jonathan B. Spira, an analyst at the business research firm Basex, estimated that extreme multitasking—information overload—costs the US economy $650 billion a year in lost productivity.

When psychologist René Marois of Vanderbilt University used fMRI scans, he found evidence of a "response selection bottleneck" that occurs when the brain is forced to respond to several stimuli at once. Task switching leads to time lost as the brain determines which task to perform.

While you might believe that it speeds you up, in fact, the more you try to multitask, the slower and less effective you become—as much as 40 per cent slower, according to an American study reported in the *Journal of Experimental Psychology*.

What's more, according to Russell Poldrack, psychology professor at the University of California in Los Angeles, "Multitasking adversely affects how you learn." Even if you can absorb information while distracted by different sources, "learning is less flexible and more specialized, so you cannot retrieve the information as easily," Professor Poldrack found. fMRI scans reveal that people use different areas of the brain for learning and storing new information when they are distracted, which limits how much you can retrieve and use. Discussing his research on multitasking on National Public Radio recently, Poldrack warned, "We have to be aware that there is a cost to the way that our society is changing, that humans are not built to work this way. We're really built to focus."

Now the upside. It turns out that focus—intense, full-immersion focus—is extremely healthy, perhaps even essential to your learning and happiness. Earlier we mentioned the ancient state of *yu*. Another resource is the modernized landmark book *Flow*, written by one of the top thinkers of our time, Mihaly Csikszentmihalyi. Both reveal how those moments when we get lost in the task at hand, forget time or our surroundings and are completely enthralled with the challenge are for many people among the most fulfilling moments in one's life. They also appear to have a positive effect on your health, energy and optimism. So, in short, focus is good. And as both ancient and modern teachers point out, *yu,* or deep immersion focus, can be learned, even mastered.

The key is to become "autotelic", which Csikszentmihalyi explains comes from the Greek "auto" for self and "telic" for goal. Work offers the most naturally rewarding experience when it becomes something you are pursuing for its own sake. Csikszentmihalyi quotes surgeons who say of their work, "It is so enjoyable that I would do it even if I didn't have to," and sailors who say, "I am spending a lot of money and time on this boat, but it is worth it—nothing quite compares with the feeling I get when I am out sailing."

Of course, not all work offers the same opportunity for this kind of experience. In general, and with some notable exceptions, there is a big difference between someone working as a brain surgeon and another person doing particularly routine hard labour or working on a monotonous assembly line: the brain surgeon has a chance to learn new things every day, and every day he learns that he is in control and that he can perform difficult tasks. The "shovel that pile of dirt" labourer is forced to repeat the same exhausting motions over and over again, and what he learns is mostly about his own helplessness. Yet mindset can help you transform your relationship to work.

INTENSITY BUILDERS

The rarer something is, the more valuable it becomes. In fact, that is one of the driving principles of this book. All the elements of the 3G Mindset are becoming more rare, but at the same time they are increasingly needed by employers. This "rare-equals-precious" principle especially applies to focus. If you're the one fit person at the beach, you stand out in a good way.

The same can be said for being the person on the team or in the business with an uncommon ability to remain fully focused on the task or conversation while others' attention flits around like a caffeinated gnat. In a relatively short time, your focus can dramatically improve. Focus fuels productivity and, in extreme cases, can even save lives!

THE REAL STORY—INTENSITY BUILDER

As cops, we're expected and trained to shut out all distractions, focus intently on our surroundings and constantly scan for even the smallest detail out of the ordinary. Doing it right requires incredible intensity. At first, like most people, I was pretty poor at it. Most of the more seasoned cops spotted things I missed, right in front of my face. They'd tease us pretty relentlessly over our blind spots. But over a relatively short time, it's amazing how skilled you can get at deep focus.

The day I realized I had "graduated" from being a rookie observer was the day I was in an unmarked vehicle with a guy from the Detective Bureau. We were returning from a court appearance and we got behind a green Cadillac. There were two men in the vehicle and as we pulled up to a light we stopped directly behind the car. I noticed that the licence plate was secured at the bottom by two screws.

What caught my eye was that the area around the top two screw holes was very clean. In fact, it led me to believe that the plate had very recently been secured at the top. Well, anyway,

we ran the plate [had it checked out] and it came back that it should be on another vehicle that was reported stolen from the local train station. When we got a marked car into position for back-up, we stopped the vehicle and took down the thugs. It turned out that they were both armed with guns, and one was wanted on an out-of-state warrant. Deep focus can really pay off.
— Duane Giannini, former police officer

You can apply some of the same principles to strengthening your focus that officers in the line of fire use to improve theirs. Try these three intensity builders:

1. **Nail the Details.** This intensity builder is like a grown-up version of the game I Spy. Look for the "licence plate screws" that you would otherwise miss. As people talk to you, look for hidden details on their faces, in their clothing or surroundings.

Pretend you're in a spy movie. You're about to be kidnapped and blindfolded. What details around you would you wish you had noticed that a non-spy might otherwise miss?

In any meeting—perhaps the most commonly cited source of utter boredom for many people—what do you notice about how the setting (lights, seating, room, vibe, etc.) affects the energy and interaction in the room? How do vocal tones affect the quality and energy of interaction?

2. **Do the 3G Scan.** Every time you are with or you speak to another person, try to instantly assess their three Gs: global, good and grit. Which one's strongest? Which is weakest? If you were to assign a score of 1 to 10 to each, what would it be? How quickly can you guess? What did they say or do that led to your conclusions? What subtle clues and cues do they offer?

Mastering this skill has the double pay-off of enhancing your intensity while deepening your understanding of the 3Gs. If you become an expert at spotting cues in others, you can do the same for yourself.

3. **Create the Cone of Silence.** This is about what you create inside, not what exists outside. Many people require uninterrupted, utter silence in order to concentrate. The reality is that few workplaces offer such a luxury. Most people are besieged with noisy distractions and interruptions, many of which may be far more interesting than completing the expense report on your computer screen. One of the amazing factors of full immersion, or the highest form of intense focus, is the ability to shut out all external stimuli and create your Zen-like focus in the midst of what may be complete chaos. This too can be practised and mastered.

Begin with light doses of distraction—like music, an open window or incoming email—that you intentionally ignore. Build your intensity and discipline by welcoming more tempting distractions that you purposely ignore, like a driver refusing to turn his head to stare at the car crash on the side of the road. Over time, you will master the classic distractions such as email, phone calls, text messages, people's voices and daily noise rather than letting them be your master. Create the cone of silence with the press of an internal button, anywhere, any time you wish.

Tenacity

Tenacity is a vital dimension of grit, one you, most likely, admire in others. It is the sheer ability to stick to it, the relentless pursuit of something most others would have given up on much sooner. And the tougher the job market gets, or the higher your goals, the more tenacity matters and the more it pays off.

> ➦Diamonds are nothing more than chunks of coal that stuck to their jobs.
> — *Malcolm Stevenson Forbes*

People with strong grit don't get offended—they get tenacious. Imagine being that phone message at the bottom of the stack. Do you play polite? Wait for that overloaded boss to find your message and return your call? Or do you become politely tenacious, setting up a regular rhythm of kind, thoughtful but fairly constant reminders that in effect say, "Hey, remember me? Please put my note back on top of the stack." Over time, whether out of guilt, frustration or impending relief, that person is likely to take or return your call, sparking the conversation that could change your life.

We know. Most of our best breakthroughs and career advances have come not through luck but through sheer resilience: grit, good and global. When Paul launched his firm PEAK Learning in 1987, he desperately wanted Deloitte (then Touche Ross) as his first client. If they said yes, he was on his way. If they said no, he could not even pay the phone bill.

It took seventeen phone calls, nine letters and five meetings, three of which he drove hours to attend only to find them cancelled at the last minute, just to get his first speaking gig with them. People told him to stop beating himself up. They tried to help Paul come to his senses and see that Deloitte clearly didn't want to talk to him, let alone hire him. But Paul chose not to take it personally, and used his polite tenacity to land his first paying client, one who has now been with him for twenty-four years.

Earlier, you learned the vital equation that it takes a strong enough *why* to really pursue anything with all your heart. Without the *why*, you won't have the *will*. And without the will, you won't.

TENACITY BUILDER—THE TENACIOUS WHY

This tool is the simplest and perhaps the most powerful for growing grit. Each time you consider going after something, whether or not it's worth another shot, or if it's best to give up, ask yourself this simple question: "What is the most compelling reason I would pursue this?" Or "What is the grander *why*?"

If your answer is compelling, it may make you stand up straighter, set your jaw and go for it with everything you have to give. If it is not, that may be an indicator that your tenacity is best funnelled towards something more important.

Elevating the why can have a profound effect. For example, if you are considering going after a specific job opportunity and a friend asks you, "Why are you thinking of doing this?", if your answer is "Because it pays more," that may or may not be compelling enough.

But if the bigger why is, "Because I could give the extra money to my mother to get some help to clean her house, which she cannot do by herself any more," then that may be a big enough why to make you do whatever it takes, or all you can do to make it happen.

The tenacious why girds your body and focuses your effort. Now imagine the uncommon success you can enjoy when you jolt your brain to bust through any remaining barriers.

Microchallenge:
The Tenacious Why

1

Pick something towards which you are currently or would like soon to be putting a great deal of effort.

A. _____

_____

_____

_____

_____

2

Ask yourself, "Why do I want to do this?"

A. _____

_____

_____

_____

_____

3

Repeat the question "Yes, but why?" until you get to what is the highest, most compelling, most definite reason, the one that galvanizes you to give your utter best.

A. _____

_____

_____

_____

_____

4

Do this for any potentially exhausting effort you put into anything.

TENACITY BUILDER—BRAIN JOLTERS

This tool is shockingly simple and even more shockingly effective. It is based on the principle that one of the most direct ways to shift your hard-wiring is simply to jolt it out of its track. Weak grit is usually caused by weak assumptions. The assumptions spawn from your hard-wired pattern of response to whatever is happening. Like deep ruts in the road, you naturally follow the weak assumption path. Then you jerk the wheel and jolt your tyres out of the rut to higher ground and a freer path.

Here are a couple of our favourites. When faced with an impossibility, ask:

Clearly, this is impossible. But if it were possible, how would I/you/we do it?

Clearly, this can't be done. But if it could, how would we I/you/we do it?

You can customize the wording to the situation. The main idea is to acknowledge the reality then shatter it with the possibility of provocation.

Brain Jolter Questions
Examples:

1

So there's clearly no way to get a passport from you in one day. But if I could, how would we do it?

2

So you cannot accommodate me at your hotel tonight. But if you could, how would you do it?

3

So you can't give me an interview. I understand. But if you could, how could we make it happen?

4

I'll clearly never get this job. But if I could, how would I make it happen?

5

There is no money to give me the rise you feel I deserve. Can't happen, the money doesn't exist. But if it did, where could we find it?

6

So you simply won't consider someone with my background. I understand. But if you did, how could we make that happen?

This simple question, which can be asked in endless ways, has been used to create genuine breakthroughs in the face of seemingly rock-solid impossibilities. Some of the challenges we've used Brain Jolters for include:

- Getting a new passport in one day when it was supposed to take at least six weeks
- Getting hotel rooms in completely oversold hotels
- Getting seats on planes when none exist
- Winning client engagements when we didn't meet the original qualifications, and were denied consideration
- Meeting with people we were told one cannot meet
- Gaining access to special places that it is forbidden to enter
- Getting banks to reconsider their new iron-clad rules on loans
- Helping friends, clients and protégés make impossible dreams possible
- And, upon reflection, probably when we each got our respective wives to say, "Yes, I will marry you!"

Grit can really pay off. And you can use it to bust through any obstacle you face in your efforts to get or keep the best job.

Microchallenge:
Brain Jolter

1

Pick an obstacle you recently faced or currently confront. Pick something you want which most people might consider impossible.

A. _____

_____

_____

_____

_____

2

What would be the normal or expected response?

A. _____

_____

_____

_____

3

Say, "Clearly, this cannot be done. But if it could, how would I/we do it?"

A. _____

_____

_____

_____

4

Now that you've done this in your head, go and do it for real. We dare you.

Here's the gist. By jolting your brain or jolting someone else's with one of these questions, you remove the No Entry sign from the road and open new terrain. Brain Jolters can be used for the most mundane and the most profound obstacles. And it is shocking how frequently and how well they work within yourself and with others.

The Grit Game

You don't have to rely on the growing mass of groundbreaking research to prove that grit matters. It just makes sense. You can't help but be drawn and attracted to people who have mindsets that exude growth, resilience, intensity and tenacity. You trust them to get things done, you want them on your team, especially when the going gets tough, and you admire their capacity to make the impossible possible. You probably notice other people consider those with great grit lucky. But you know better. You know this is not some magic twist of their DNA.

You may recall from earlier in this chapter that grit can not only be measured, it can be permanently and endlessly improved. You also know that grit, while vital, is not enough.

People with greater grit, especially when combined with global and good, are more successful. Overall, they are healthier and happier, as well as more agile, innovative, optimistic, productive, resilient, tenacious and engaged in anything they choose to pursue. They tend to be higher performers, promoted faster and often paid more because they contribute more and generate more value.

And there is no reason that the person you admire for exceptional mindset—grit, good and global—can't be you. Employ the tools you learned in this and the preceding chapters, and you will be well on your way to getting and keeping the job you want.

➡ **Grit:**
The fuel cell of your 3G Mindset. It spurs you on when others give up and gives you the grip you need to forge ahead. Grit proves that anyone can come out on top.

CHAPTER RECAP

Your grit comprises growth, resilience, intensity and tenacity and you can use different tools to improve these aspects of your mindset.

Optimizers
Use these questions in any situation to help you create an immediate shift to a growth mindset.

CORE Questions
Use these scientifically grounded questions to create breakthroughs and demonstrate uncommon resilience in any situation, for any adversity or opportunity.

Intensity Builders
Remember to follow the three steps to really build your intensity. (1) nail the details, (2) do the 3G scan and (3) create the cone of silence.

Brain Jolters
Use these "jerk the wheel" questions to create possibilities that otherwise would not exist.

8

GET THE
BEST JOBS,
THE 3G WAY

We know what we are, but not what we may be
— *William Shakespeare*

The world's top employers know what they want. But they don't know how to get it. They desperately need your help. They know the ways they select and grow their people have gaping flaws. They default to skill set as their hiring criterion when they really crave the right mindset.

So how do you help employers see your strong 3G Mindset? How do you make it glaringly obvious in your CV, during your interview and on the job—in every task, challenge and interaction?

This chapter shows you how. Apply the tips on the following pages and you will literally triple your chances of getting the job you want and become one of the most valued (and promotable) employees at any level in the organization.

Triple Your Chances of Landing the Best Job

In the moment of truth, who gets the job? Who succeeds, and who doesn't? Specifically, what makes the defining difference?

To set you apart, we'll shatter some common advice and give you a golden breakthrough to make your CV truly shine.

It all began by comparing who wins and who loses at the CV game. We put together a groundbreaking study and discovered some shocking truths about some of the standard rules for CVs. And we hit upon a real breakthrough that triples your chances of getting the job. We'll explain these in sequence. First, we must confront the brutal reality.

The Brutal Reality about CVs

It's sobering. CVs matter. That you know. But, more than ever in this global, connected world, those who make the hiring decisions rely on your CV to decide if you're in or out. Generally, that person will make a decision about you in a few seconds.

Your goal is to give them something in your CV that warrants a second (and third) glance. You want them to pause and give you serious consideration. You have to stand out from the pack, or the game's over.

Employers told us a disturbing truth. Because they mostly dread the arduous task of trawling through big stacks of CVs, they begin by looking for any reason to reject you in a minute or less. Most have their own personal list of pet peeves that creates an instant "reject". But it gets worse. With the increased use of the miniscreen (smartphones, etc.), they see less and miss more, making it even tougher to have them appreciate all you have to offer.

Given the brutal reality, who wins? Who loses? We designed and commissioned an independent study to find out.

The Winning CV Study

We recognized that we were in a unique position to get past all the "how to get the best job" mythology and finally pinpoint exactly what does and does not make employers pick you over everyone else. So we did.

Given REED's position as a global recruiter with a fifty-year history, whose online job board, reed.co.uk, is Europe's largest, attracting more than 20 million applications each year, we were able to analyse who gets the job and who doesn't by tapping the hundreds of thousands of individual CVs we track each year.

In simple terms, here's what we did.

1. We selected 30,000 diverse CVs (various jobs, years, levels)
2. We divided our sample into two main groups, the winners and the losers, those who got the job and those who didn't
3. A team of independent researchers analysed the differences

What we discovered will forever change the way you craft your CV. Consider what doesn't work, and then, what *does*.

The Findings. False Advice—What Doesn't Work

Consider these three common tips offered in many job-search guides:

1. Start your CV with a personal profile or personal statement
2. Use active verbs
3. Include hobbies and interests

It turns out these tactics actually give no advantage whatsoever. This is not just our opinion. It is simply a cold, hard fact gleaned from a large independent study. Here's what we discovered.

1. Personal Profile or Statement: Sometimes called "personal statements", "impact statements" or "pen profiles", these are those statements, just a few sentences long, usually found at the start of the CV. They offer a short, snappy summary of what you have to offer an employer.

> **"Their" Advice:** Include a personal statement or profile to help you really shine and give the employer a chance to know you better.

Our Findings: 83 per cent of the sample of winners and losers included "personal statements", usually at the start of CVs. However, there is no significant correlation with success. *Personal statements make no difference.*

2. Active Verbs: These include words such as "managed", "led", "coordinated", "communicated", "created" and "delivered".

"Their" Advice: Active verbs make all the difference. Use the lists provided in the career advice books, and you will have a real edge.

Our Findings: On average within the 30,000 CVs, each one included three active verbs. Both winners and losers had them, but there was no correlation with success. *Active verbs make no difference.*

3. Hobbies and Interests: These are statements or lists that show your pursuits outside of work, reflecting how well rounded and/or interesting you may be.

"Their" Advice: This is an essential way for the employer to know you better, providing a chance to show other sides of yourself.

Our Findings: 62 per cent of the database of the winners and losers included "other interest" or "hobbies" sections, usually at the end of CVs. There is no significant correlation with success. *Hobbies and interests make no difference.*

So if these supposedly sacred rules of winning CVs don't actually make a difference, what does separate the winners from the losers? And what, if any, role does 3G really play?

The Triple-Your-Chances Strategy

The 3G Mindset triples your chances of winning the job. Through our research we discovered that evidencing 3G Mindset makes a powerful difference to a job seeker's prospects.

Here's how. We found that the winning formula is to create statements that demonstrate how you have put specific 3G Mindset qualities into practice to achieve tangible results. We call this formulation "3G Mindset at Work". People who do this quite literally triple their chances of getting the job they want:

$$3G\ Mindset\ at\ Work =$$
$$3G\ Mindset\ Quality \rightarrow Put\ into\ Practice \rightarrow to\ Achieve\ a\ Result.$$

For example, compare:

Losing Entry:	Responsible for IT strategy and team meetings
Winning Entry:	Created a new, global team of diverse IT professionals to develop innovative solutions to our most persistent IT problems
Losing Entry:	Operated a forklift and inventory tracking system
Winning Entry:	In response to the frustrations reflected in the employee survey, I generated five ways to significantly enhance the efficiency and accuracy of the inventory management process

Look at these examples through your expert 3G lens. In both cases, the first is flat, mildly informative at best, and uninteresting. There is no vitality, no 3G Mindset quality and no real result. The second reflects one or more mindset qualities off the master list that were put into practice to achieve an impressive result. It doesn't just use active verbs; it puts an activity into context.

Let's analyse a couple more examples:

> Losing Entry: Supervised customer service team for retail operations
>
> Winning Entry: Coordinated and led the customer service team to improve customer satisfaction for retail operations by 29 per cent in six months by harvesting best practices from unrelated industries

---

What makes the second entry so much more effective?

3G Mindset Qualities (implied or stated)—collaboration, empathy, flexible, creative, tenacity, growth, intensity, boundaryless, broad-minded (and more)

Put in Practice—pace (six months), tangible improvement (29 per cent), engaging others (leading, coordinating)

Achieve a Result—29 per cent in six months. Impressive!

> Losing Entry: Provided accounting services to several internal customers
>
> Winning Entry: Fended off the threat of having my function outsourced by pinpointing and resolving the top five internal customer finance-related frustrations by the end of the first year

3G Mindset Qualities (implied or stated)—Curious, open-minded, empathetic, dependable, intense, growth, tenacity (and more)

Put in Motion—Pace (first year), tangible improvement (top five frustrations), committed (pinpointed and resolved)

Achieve a Result—Resolved top five by end of the first year

Specificity also matters. The winning 3G Mindset-infused examples gave specific details of what it was the individuals had accomplished. Usually these details included actions, names and numbers. The more compelling the examples, the more convincing the evidence of just how someone's 3G Mindset affected his or her behaviour and success at work.

Our analysis revealed that CVs that show one or more examples of 3G Mindset at work are **three times** more likely to get the job. That's the minimum. People who used two or more examples of 3G Mindset at work on their CVs were *five times more likely to get the job*. The statistics don't lie. In a sense, this startling conclusion had been staring us in the face all along. It is the combination of 3G Mindset qualities and action that makes an individual attractive to prospective employers, because one without the other is like a wheel without an axle. Mindset words by themselves and mindset in general mean little. It is only when the 3G Mindset is shown to be at work that the rubber really hits the road.

Providing evidence of 3G Mindset at work is not complicated to do, and it brings CVs to life. It provides the necessary detail that establishes your authenticity. It helps your prospective employer to visualize what you have done and to get a real sense of the mindset you bring, which the employer clearly values. It gives employers a sense of who you really are and what you are made of.

3G Mindset at Work—Losing vs. Winning Statements	
Losing CV	**Winning CV**
Responsible for IT strategy and team meetings	Created a new, global team of diverse IT professionals to develop innovative solutions to their most persistent IT problems. *Potential 3G descriptors: open, global, tenacious, collaborative, intense, resilient, curious, agile*
Operated a forklift and inventory tracking system	In response to the frustrations reflected in the employee survey, I generated five ways to significantly enhance the efficiency and accuracy of the inventory management process. *Potential 3G descriptors: intense, growth, collaborative, accountable, empathetic*

3G Mindset at Work—Losing vs. Winning Statements	
Losing CV	**Winning CV**
Supervised customer service team for retail operations	Coordinated and led the customer service team to improve customer satisfaction for retail operations by 29 per cent in six months by harvesting best practices from unrelated industries. *Potential 3G descriptors: empathy, collaboration, flexible, tenacity, growth, intensity, boundaryless, broad-minded*
Provided accounting services to several internal customers	Fended off the threat of having my function outsourced by pinpointing and resolving the top five internal customer finance-related frustrations by the end of the first year. *Potential 3G descriptors: curious, empathy, dependable, intense, growth, tenacity, open-minded*

The 3G Mindset at Work Acid Test

You can go beyond the basic criteria—3G in practice with results—with the 3G Mindset at work acid test. A good way to test the strength of your 3G Mindset at work statement is by asking this question: *based on only this statement, what three words would I use to describe this person?* Your answer, if honest, should sound like 3G qualities, right off the list.

You will recall that both winning and losing entries had hobbies or interests. Having this section gives no natural advantage. But doing it right can be a big boost.

Consider this losing CV's entry in the hobbies and interests section:

Running, travel, reading, sports

The actual winning entry (for an accounting job) was:

Exercise is an important aspect within my life. I like to set goals both physically and mentally for myself, attending the gym three times a week in preparation for the cancer research run that I will be taking part in later this year.

Now apply the 3G Mindset at work acid test: which three words would you use to describe this person, based on this statement? (Potential descriptors are "intense", "focused", "growing", "compassionate", "committed", "sincere".)

Here's another:

| Losing Entry: | Experience working with IT professionals at all levels |
| Winning Entry: | Created and chaired the Information Security and Assurance Forum—an informal body of top information security officers from large multinational corporations with IT support centres (with a complete list of the top global corporations involved included) |

This "normal" statement in the losing entry indicates this person's basic skill but totally lacks any 3G. No 3G qualities put to work to create results are provided. In short, this does not show 3G Mindset at work. It is simply a vague, uncompelling and unsubstantiated assertion.

So how do you immediately grab this opportunity? The good news is that most of your Gen G competition will continue to produce CVs much as they have done for decades, following discredited conventions and clinging desperately to the hope that somebody out there will see them for who they really are. What if you could escape the straitjacket of the past and take advantage of an altogether better way for you to present yourself for any opportunity you seek? You can.

CMe

The CMe reinvents and replaces the CV. It provides the information and insights into you that employers want. It infuses and highlights your mindset strengths throughout in a way no standard document can.

Based on this initial 3G Mindset at work breakthrough, we brainstormed to provide you with an even better breakthrough in the form of a powerful tool. We recognized the need for an entirely new way to present yourself and your 3G Mindset to those who might affect your future. Employers are begging for it. You need a powerful way to give them what they want.

If the current CV format, like the original X-ray, typically provides an inadequate low-resolution and two-dimensional impression of an individual's qualities and achievements, how might we develop it to actually provide a truer three-dimensional, high-resolution picture of a person who employers, not to mention the people themselves, appear to be crying out for?

We have created the CMe in response to this glaringly apparent gap in the market. We want to help you multiply your chances of success, allowing employers to view you in a much more positive and meaningful light.

CMe

The Next Generation, High-Definition CV

CMe is the only tool in existence that highlights your 3G Mindset along with your qualifications and vital information to provide the 360-degree, "high-def" picture of you employers crave.

The CMe truly is three-dimensional. Online, it will give you a three-dimensional representation of yourself in a way that will resonate with employers, 97 per cent of whom say they favour mindset over skill set. Or you can print your CMe for those times where having one in hand is essential.

The evidence of your 3G Mindset at work will automatically fall into one of the 3Gs: global, good or grit. This is an important point to remember.

Microchallenge:
3G Mindset

1

Write down the three specific qualities (under each) that you are most proud of related to global, good and grit.

2

Identify times at and beyond work when you have actively used those qualities or put your 3G Mindset to work.

3

Create your authentic 3G stories and examples. Draft the most compelling sentence for each.

4

Challenge yourself to build your 3G Mindset bank. Build your list under each heading to a total of at least ten statements.

5

Select the most relevant (to you and your potential employer) and compelling examples to include in your new CMe.

Or complete this challenge as part of building your personal CMe at www.3GMindset.com/book.

Craft Your Own CMe and Land the Job You Want

Developing a strong and compelling CMe is the next step as you *Put Your Mindset to Work*. In contrast to the traditional CV, your CMe includes and highlights:

- Your 3G Panorama results, featuring your 3G Mindset strengths and preferences
- A bank of specific examples of 3G Mindset at work from which you can select to customize each job inquiry
- Required skills and qualifications

This gives the employer what he or she wants, a direct insight into the 3G Mindset qualities you both value most and demonstrate best. It makes you shine and helps strengthen your chances of finding both a good job and a good fit.

A well-crafted CMe will help you to instantly stand apart from others with similar or even superior skills and experience. It uniquely draws from and links into your 3G Panorama results and, of course, highlights your experience, education and skill set in a new way that demonstrates 3G Mindset at work. We will show you how to apply your 3G Mindset to create your own personalized CMe, and this in turn will help you land that job you want.

Creating your CMe is straightforward, but it will take time and it requires your intense attention. You will be creating a high-definition representation of yourself and you will want to make sure that it is exactly right.

You can begin to create your CMe manually, or you can create and complete it using the CMe feature online at no charge. Either way, to build your CMe, you will need the results from your 3G Panorama.

Online CMe

You can access and transfer the results of your 3G Panorama automatically into your CMe template with a simple click when you complete the panorama or indeed afterwards by directly accessing your personal data section. You will also need to include your personal details and a summary of your skills, education and experience. You will be able to do a lot of this directly from your existing CV or, alternatively, you can create something completely new. In many ways, approaching your CMe with fresh eyes and through the specific lens of your 3G Mindset is a distinct advantage because your 3G qualities will more likely shine through.

You create your CMe in five easy steps:

1. Complete your 3G Panorama report
2. Input your personal data in section two
3. Input your key skills inventory and qualifications in section three
4. Input your career history in section four
5. Fine-tune, review and incorporate 3G Mindset at work examples

Here's how to link from your 3G Panorama to inform the creation of your CMe. Go back to your personal account on www.3GMindset.com. Once you have completed your 3G Panorama, you will see a tab that says "Create CMe". Clicking on this button will pull your 3G scores from your 3G Panorama into a new template in which you can create your CMe. Follow the steps to include your key skills and qualifications and, most important, to add examples and evidence of your 3G Mindset strengths and 3G Mindset at work.

Note: The CMe design program will guide you not just to insert but to infuse the best of your 3G Mindset throughout your CMe, so your mindset strengths shine through.

Preparing to Create Your CMe

If you want to start preparing your CMe now, you can take the following steps:

1. Gather a summary of your skills, education and experience. You may have this prewritten from your prior CV.

2. Write down your personal information (name, address, contact information, etc.). Again, you may have this on an existing CV.
3. Print your 3G Panorama results and report.
4. Take your list of 3G Mindset at work examples from the challenge on page 203.
5. Circle every spot on your existing documents (cover letter, CV, etc.) where you could replace a word, phrase or entry with a 3G Mindset quality demonstrated by an example of your 3G Mindset at work. You should, in any case, make sure your existing CV demonstrates these 3G Mindset at work examples, regardless of whether or not you choose to create your own CMe.

Taking these steps will shorten the time you will need online to create your personal CMe.

Invest your best in this effort. It may take you a little while to complete but, at the end of it, you will be ready to go online to create your very own CMe, exactly what top employers have told you (and us) they wholeheartedly prefer. Once you fill in your information online, your CMe will be instantly ready for you to present to prospective employers in either printed or, ideally, virtual form, so you can at least triple your chances that they choose you. Increasingly, your CMe can replace and surpass your CV, setting you apart. Ultimately, it will save you time and fuel your opportunities.

Microchallenge:
CMe

1 Go to www.3GMindset.com and log into your personal account and click on "CMe". If you have not yet created your account, go to www.3GMindset.com/book.

2 Click "Share" and add a request for feedback message, and share your CMe with friends, colleagues and family.

3 Use their feedback to make it even stronger.

CMe Tips

To get the greatest benefit as you do this, it is essential that you are accurate and honest. Your CMe will be a high-definition, three-dimensional picture of yourself. What's most important is that it is authentic and not a fake. It is highly likely that your CMe will be packed full of examples, but you must ensure that the examples you ultimately choose are true to who you are and what you did. They should be the ones that you are most happy and confident talking about. Try to highlight your key achievements without exaggerating the circumstances, and always look for ways to demonstrate your 3G Mindset at work.

Your CMe is primarily designed to dramatically improve the odds that you land on your prospective employer's short list. You will then have an opportunity to further sell your 3G Mindset strengths in the interview. Your CMe will give you the perfect foundation to expand upon when you are speaking face to face with your potential employer. It will be a talking point and you will have provided your interviewer with much more information about yourself and your mindset than other applicants will have done. You will be the only one who clearly communicates and provides what employers desperately want. Above all, you will stand out.

CMe™

How Does CMe Differ from a Traditional CV?

Research has clearly indicated that employers value mindset over skill set. The CMe replaces the outdated, traditional CV by including and infusing this vital ingredient, providing a much more detailed and valuable insight into the job candidate.

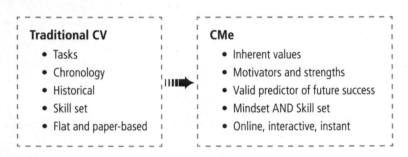

Traditional CV	CMe
• Tasks	• Inherent values
• Chronology	• Motivators and strengths
• Historical	• Valid predictor of future success
• Skill set	• Mindset AND Skill set
• Flat and paper-based	• Online, interactive, instant

The CMe is weighted towards the missing ingredient—mindset. It provides the individual's essential validated 3G Panorama scores alongside key mindset values and strengths, as well as authentic examples of mindset at work.

CMe – The Next Generation CV
Edward P. Robinson

Edward received an above average score on 3G Panorama.

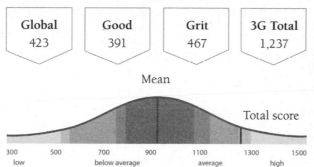

Global	Good	Grit	3G Total
423	391	467	1,237

Your 3G Panorama scores are loaded in from your online assessment.

Mindset Qualities

Edward's 3G Panorama profile showed that his three areas of strength are:

- Grit – Resilience
- Global – Openness
- Good – Integrity

Edward selected the following six mindset qualities as the most important to him:

- Honest
- Loyal
- Flexible
- Adaptable
- Innovative
- Sincere

Enter the mindset qualities that are most important to you. There is a tool on the website to help you to do this.

3G Mindset at Work

- I conduct market reviews and make recommendations based on a client's financial and medical situation in an FSA-regulated and highly targeted environment. I also maintain this portfolio of clients, monitoring and creating opportunities for cross-sales within the group.

- I have experience working in a contact centre, working under extremely high call volumes, both

Enter the top three examples of how you have used your 3G Mindset to achieve demonstrable results.

selling new policies and servicing existing ones.
I am able to deal with a wide variety of customers,
each with different needs and requirements.

- I am a trombonist and used to be a member of the
Regional Symphony Orchestra. I now volunteer with
the Civic Youth Orchestra, assisting with sectional
tuition and filling in for the brass section when
required.

Introducing Yourself Effectively

When you first contact your prospective employer, whether you do so by email or by mail, and whether you are sending a traditional application form, your CV, or your new CMe, you will need some well-chosen words to accompany your application and grab the employer's interest.

This is the cover letter. It is another opportunity to offer something powerful and personal that will make you stand out. Think carefully about the job you are applying for and which specific 3G Mindset qualities will be most important.

Consider the different contexts and situations the role might involve you in, and then pick the most appropriate 3G Mindset at work examples that you have developed. Make sure that they are compelling and relevant. Then highlight them in your cover letter.

Do not try to reproduce the effect of your entire CMe. One or two examples of your 3G Mindset at work combined with an obvious interest in and enthusiasm for the organization you are applying for will greatly improve your odds of making the short list for an interview. In this simple way, you can easily show your 3G Mindset at work in your letter.

3G MINDSET AT WORK COVER LETTER: EXAMPLE

Dear (named employer contact)
Customer Service Team Leader

   I am writing in response to your advertisement for the above position.

   Your commitment to the highest levels of customer service and your emphasis on continual innovation to stay ahead of your competitors, as detailed on your website, make me especially interested in applying for this role.

   In my current position, I have:

   • *Coordinated and led the customer service team to improve customer satisfaction for retail operations by 29 per cent in six months by implementing ideas from unrelated industries.*
   • *Analysed employee feedback and generated five ways to significantly enhance the efficiency and accuracy of management processes.*
   • *Helped build team morale and supported a good cause by organizing and completing a company half-marathon for cancer research.*

   I enclose what many employers consider the next-generation CV, called a "CMe", for your consideration, and very much look forward to hearing from you.

                             Yours sincerely,
                             David Barrow

Microchallenge:
3G Mindset Cover Letter

1 For any job, pick the mindset qualities you believe to be most important for that job.

2 From your list of 3G Mindset strengths (3G Panorama) and the list of 3G Mindset at work examples, pick the two or three you think will best fit that specific opportunity.

3 Highlight these in your cover letter, so the prospective employer gets an initial glimpse of your 3G Mindset at work.

Demonstrating Your 3G Mindset in an Interview

Now that you have created your CMe and used it, the big day has come. You have been invited to the all-important interview for that job you really want. How can you best demonstrate your 3G Mindset at work in the interview and how can you ensure that you not only impress but also stand out and secure that job offer?

Tip 1: Remember: no matter what questions the interviewer is asking, he or she is desperately looking for evidence of your 3G Mindset.

Tip 2: Interviewers are unlikely to use the term "mindset" or know what to ask or look for. You can introduce the topic by asking them to think about whether they value skill set or mindset more.

Tip 3: Authentically infuse every statement you make with some facet of 3G.

This is what employers want. We surveyed thousands, and their message is clear.

Compare the answers to this interviewer's question or challenge:

"We have 250 applicants. Tell me why I should pick you for this job."

1. "I have all the skills and qualifications you are looking for. In fact, I have two years of experience that are directly relevant to this job. If you'd like, I can describe the tasks and responsibilities of my former jobs in more detail."
2. "At its heart this job seems to be about solving complex problems and not getting beaten down by constant change. That requires curiosity and resilience, both traits that I have demonstrated in my CV. I would like to tell you about what I did in my last job to show you that I'm the kind of person who is fuelled by tough challenges. That's why I applied for this job."

Which candidate would *you* choose? The first puts you in the middle of the pack. The second sets you apart, with facts.

You will soon discover that it is an easy and enjoyable challenge to infuse your 3G Mindset into every answer you give and every question you ask.

Employers will question your 3G Mindset in many different ways. But, ultimately, knowledge is power, and understanding what an employer is actually looking for through the barrage of confusing questions and the battery of assessments will really give you the edge.

It is worth realizing just how much power you have in the interview and how comparatively little power the interviewer holds. Remember that this employer really does want to recruit someone effective. A bad hire has the potential to damage their company and to ruin the interviewer's reputation. It's his or her worst nightmare.

The person or people facing you at that first interview will know very little about you. They want to find proof that you are who you say you are. They want to see evidence that you can do what they want you to do. And although you may not have much sympathy with their fears, as you fight to deal with your own nerves, it will certainly be helpful for you to take them into account.

No matter how good a picture your CMe provides, it is only by meeting you in person that the recruiter will see the whole you. You should expect a good interviewer to use the CMe as a springboard. Recruiters will take every opportunity to probe you, and your evidence must stack up.

One recruiter with many years of experience hiring staff for a global investment bank told us how he likes to probe for tenacity and authenticity. "When I'm interviewing a potential employee, the first thing I ask about is the individual's interests. This is because their response will often show how honest they are and how passionate they are. I once interviewed someone who stated that his interest was human rights. When I asked him about it, it turned out that he had been on one march some time ago, that he hadn't done anything much since and he wasn't currently involved in the human rights movement at all. I wasn't impressed. The answer suggested to me that he was half-hearted and lacked the passion that I was looking for in the role."

Simply by asking a couple of questions about an individual's interests, this recruiter has quickly established an opinion about the job seeker's good qualities (honesty) and his grit qualities (passion, commitment, tenacity). As more and more recruiters get training in the 3G Mindset, you can expect them to focus their questions accordingly, which of course will only work to your advantage! As you can tell from the many examples provided in this book, we are already seeing the skill-set-to-mindset shift taking place.

Most interviewers are fumbling in the dark when it comes to mindset. They are going by gut or worse. They may simply resort to skill set because having competency grids and lists gives them a false sense of rigour. Remember that they desperately want the right mindset; they just may not know exactly what it is or how to ask you about it. You can change the game by giving them what they want. Through your CMe, our tips and all you've learned in this book, you will show them how. And when you do, you will shine.

One powerful and simple additional tip is simply to review the top six and top twenty mindset qualities (chapter 1) and do everything in your power to be or exude those qualities in each interview you go to. Let them haunt you in a positive way by reminding you what that prospective employer most likely seeks in you. You can hardly go wrong with the top six.

How does this information help you? First of all, it underlines again just how important it is to be authentic, particularly on your CMe. Just as high-definition television makes it hard for actors to hide scars, exaggerating your interests and achievements or inventing details about what you have done on your CMe is a recipe for disaster. It's just that much easier to spot.

In contrast, where you have used genuine examples of 3G qualities at work and built on real achievements, questions about these will hold no fear for you. And, yes, it is well worth reminding yourself of the details underpinning some of your assertions before going for an interview. If asked, you want to be able to explain and expand upon each point.

However, the interviewer wants to tap into your genuine engagement in your examples together with your ability to expand upon them in response to a whole range of probing questions. The interviewer seeks to confirm and better understand the 3G insights about you that he or she might have gained through your CMe. With each question, your strongest mindset qualities should continue to shine. Embed them in your language. Mindset and language are like mirrors of each other. They each reflect and, to some degree, create the other.

REED's director of HR, Ian Nicholas, says: "In almost any role, I think mindset overtakes experience. If people have the right mindset, then they're going to be much more committed to their work, and they're going to gain the knowledge anyway. So if you're looking for somebody who's going to do an exceptional job for you, especially long term, I pick mindset. With the right mindset, I always think they're going to learn the knowledge over time."

Ian went on to tell us that mindset qualities and specificity go together. This is a good tip as you prepare for interviews. "When I ask competency-based questions, I also ask for evidence of real engagement.

Most people, especially at a more senior level, will give a good answer, so I do dig for genuine evidence of the specifics of the situation and the struggles they went through to implement and deliver. When someone tells me they've put a procedure in place, I would say, 'So what was the actual head-count growth, what was the percentage, which area of the business was affected and by how much?' The ones that weren't that engaged tend not to know the details. They would go, 'Oh I don't actually remember.' For me, that suggests they perhaps weren't there. I find the people who are really committed will know a lot of detail about a situation and the company, as well as the struggles they had to tenaciously endure to deliver their results. Because they were so into it they will know all the answers and communicate them with the natural passion and energy we seek in our people."

The Interviewers' Secret World

There is another aspect of the interview process that you should also keep in mind. While recruiters ultimately seek people with the 3G Mindset, they can certainly be distracted by other considerations. The important requirement not only to be fair in the recruitment process but also to be seen as fair can sometimes distort things and turn the process into a checklist activity where generating the right paperwork begins to feel more important than identifying the right person.

The potentially useful process, known as "competency-based interviewing", can sometimes be applied in very much the wrong way. We have heard many horror stories of apparently robotic recruiters relying solely on stock questions and showing a complete lack of interest in the answers to know that this is the case.

If this happens to you, don't despair. You will still be at an advantage. However stuck in a rigid, unhelpful system the recruiter appears to be during your interview, you know that, ultimately, he or she is still looking for the same thing. Your job is to convince the recruiter that you have the 3G Mindset he or she seeks. And, again, the statistics don't lie. Stick to 3G and you will triple your chances of winning the job.

You need to grasp every opportunity you have to provide employers with this proof. No matter how limiting the questions they may ask, you can be expansive in your responses. Yes, you need to be appropriate and relevant in your replies because these are all-important 3G qualities. While making sure that your responses provide a succinct answer to each query, you also need to go one step further. You need to add an example or detail taken from your experience that will demonstrate your 3G Mindset at work, just as you will have done on your CMe.

A recruiter who is following a rigidly formatted interview structure might feel frustrated that it is difficult to gain the information needed to make a full assessment. Providing interviewers with proof that you have the mindset qualities they want will relieve and delight them, and will undoubtedly help you stand out in the right way.

> If the people I interview could provide me with meaningful evidence of a winning mindset, that would be game changing. It's the one thing we need most, and the thing we are worst at assessing in the people we hire. – John Suranyi, former president, DIRECTV

By now you are aware of your 3G Mindset strengths and you should have a summary of them from your 3G Panorama results. And, ideally, you have completed your CMe. Knowing and having these is vital. Putting them to use is power.

It pays to demonstrate your overall 3G Mindset in *any* situation. In a situation like the one above, you can also play to your 3G strengths and make sure that they stand out.

If, for example, you scored high on and value the empathy and compassion facets of good, it would be beneficial to ensure that these qualities authentically come across in the exercise. Perhaps you could listen to other people's views and profess your understanding, even if you then form a counterargument. Or, if you score high on intensity in grit, it would be important to demonstrate your ability to fully engage in the challenging task at hand and put all your energy into it. This increases the chances that an employer sees and chooses you for those mindset qualities you are strongest on and value most. This can have a hugely positive impact on fit.

The most important revelation for you to take away from this chapter is that you can use your 3G Mindset to dramatically strengthen your chances at every stage of the job search process. And if you apply your 3G Mindset in the specific ways we have recommended—for creating opportunities, on your CMe (upgraded CV), in the interview and, of course, at every setback, challenge and twist of events—you will multiply your chances of success dramatically.

- -

CHAPTER RECAP

When you show 3G Mindset at work, you triple your chances of getting the job.

Insert specific examples in your CV using this formula:

3G Mindset Quality → Put into Practice → to Achieve a Result.

Personal statements, active verbs and hobbies/interests make no difference on CVs.

The CMe reinvents and replaces the CV. It provides a high-def, 3-D (3G) view of the job applicant and gives you a tool to provide employers with the proof of mindset they desperately seek.

Infuse your CMe with 3G Mindset at work examples.

Proactively demonstrate 3G qualities, especially the top twenty and top six, in every interview to truly shine.

- -

But your 3G-fuelled career success doesn't stop there. Once you've used your 3G Mindset to get the job you want, a whole new world of opportunity unfolds because some of the greatest 3G power is realized when you apply all that you have learned to keeping, advancing and flourishing in every job.

9

HOW TO KEEP A GREAT JOB AND SUCCEED AT WORK THE 3G WAY

> Far and away the best prize that life has to offer is the
> chance to work hard at work worth doing.
> *— Theodore Roosevelt*

Once you have the job, it is your personal ROI (return on individual) that will shape your destiny. Think of personal ROI as the full value you personally deliver through your work. In the simplest terms, personal ROI means comparing everything you add with everything you subtract to determine how much you truly contribute. It can help you define, calculate and improve the genuine value you contribute at work. In this chapter we'll show you how.

The greater your true overall contribution relative to the entire cost of employing you, the larger your personal ROI will be. Recognizing this is vital. Letting it haunt you (in a good way) every day at work will set you apart and put you on a path towards a rewarding and enriching career. Optimize your personal ROI and you can craft your future.

That's why personal ROI is among the most important calculations employers can consider for any person in their workforce, at any stage in that person's career. It helps answer for you and for them why they should keep you over everyone else. Your personal ROI clarifies how smart your employer was to invest in you.

Regardless of whether you're an up-and-comer, a builder or a finisher, as you grow your personal ROI, you will find yourself being promoted and retained over other more "qualified" people, as well as being given the kinds of opportunities and responsibilities few others enjoy.

Your personal ROI is a percentage that can be calculated as a function of the total value of your work, ideas and impact and your total cost to your employer, as follows:

$$ROI = \frac{(work + ideas + impact - resources)}{resources} \times 100$$

My personal ROI calculator

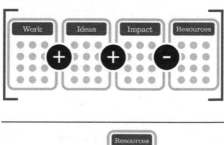

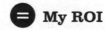

Work = Anything tangible you put effort and energy into that contributes to your organization

Ideas = These are the ideas or suggestions you offer that, when put to use, create some (hopefully positive) value for others

Impact = The net effect (plus or minus) that you have on others (see Personal Ledger and Impact Map from chapter 6)

Resources = The cost of everything provided to you and/or consumed by you at work

To understand how to determine your personal ROI, let's take a look at a few examples.

Calculating Personal ROI

Su Lim (not her real name) works as a loan officer at a mid-tier bank branch in Singapore. She has completed all of her required training and certifications to make knowledgeable assessments and recommendations regarding loan approvals and options when people come looking for money. She shows up on time, puts in her full day and rarely calls in sick. She dresses professionally, is organized and polite but is relatively low energy. Su Lim attends the required meetings and appears to be taking notes on what's decided and discussed.

At the end of the week she is pretty exhausted. If you asked her why, she would tell you it is because her boss makes her work so hard, there is too much to do and she has so many responsibilities.

Each year, her performance ratings show she is meeting expectations. The reality is that she does the job but nothing more. She has lost the original spark that made her want to help people by funding their dreams and now views loan applications as the mounting pile on her desk. As a result, clients often face delays and red tape as they await approval. But that's normal. Su Lim's processing times are in the middle of the pack. In short, *her work is average*.

When Su Lim first started with the bank, she offered several ideas for improving their rigid processes and making things more efficient for the customers. Her boss felt threatened and did not appreciate some "young kid with a college degree" trying to shake things up. So Su Lim gave up. She stopped making suggestions and became compliant. Today she attends but does not add much to meetings. If she needs an idea or answer, she consults the training manual on her shelf.

She often explains to customers why things can't be done rather than working hard to invent ways they can. Her ideas don't damage the business, but they certainly don't help. And, in a competitive business, lack of improvement usually means you are losing ground. *Su Lim scores quite low on ideas.*

On the surface, Su Lim is "impact neutral" because she is neither a serious drain upon nor a real boost to the workplace. She has her good days and bad days like everyone else. But, behind the scenes, when she and her co-workers grab lunch, or when she meets them briefly in the break room, she tends to join in and feed the griping about how upper management clearly doesn't get it when it comes to the realities of being a loan officer. In meetings, she's now the one who points out the requirements and obstacles every time someone else thinks of a better way to do something. She thinks she's doing everyone a favour but, in reality, she dampens any new sparks. *Su Lim is a negative on impact.*

Since Su Lim is paid a fair wage with benefits and has earned the standard increases in pay along the way, *her resources score would be low to moderate.*

The important thing to note is that, while Su Lim is doing well enough to remain employed (for now), and she does the required *work,* the actual value, or her personal ROI, is fairly weak.

Imagine you are her boss. If for any reason there were significant workforce reductions, would you keep Su Lim? If she asked for a promotion, would you grant the request? If you were asked to give her a reference for another job, what would you honestly say? If you were to hire someone for her job today, would you rehire Su Lim?

In our experience, and perhaps yours, we have discovered that the working world is chock-full of Su Lims. In most organizations, the majority of people do the necessary job, perceive themselves to be working very hard but, in reality, they deliver well below their potential value. As any employer will tell you, working hard is not the same as delivering optimal value.

Even without the numbers you get the sense that, although Su Lim's performance reviews claim she is meeting expectations, her personal

ROI shows she is well below potential. If you subtract everything she takes (resources, energy, momentum, possibilities) from everything she contributes (processed loans), the result is not exciting.

The personal ROI score for work, ideas and impact is determined on a scale of –20 to 20. On this scale, you might assign Su Lim a 4 on work, a –5 on ideas and a –4 on impact. Resources are determined on a scale of 0 to 20. On this scale, Su Lim might score around a 5. Plugging these scores into the formula below results in a personal ROI of –200 per cent, for a "normal" employee! Doing the job does not mean the same as delivering real value.

$$ROI = \frac{(work + ideas + impact - resources) \times 100}{Resources}$$

Su Lim's Personal ROI

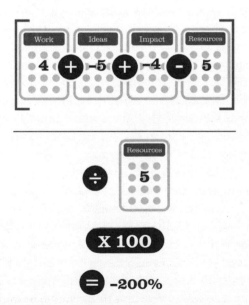

Having calculated Su Lim's personal ROI, it may be useful to delve deeper into her 3G Mindset. Use your new expertise to rate or score Su Lim's 3G Mindset. To avoid confusion with personal ROI, let's use a scale of 1 to 10, with 10 being the highest.

Begin with global. Global includes both connectivity and openness. It means considering all you do in the grander context of the economy and world. And it means having the curiosity, openness and agility to lift your eyes beyond your immediate world and reach out into the boundaryless expanse to harvest new insights and ideas. How would you score Su Lim? She goes to her bank, focuses only on what's going on within her bank and has no desire (perhaps resists efforts) to reinvent, or even improve, how she does what she does. On a scale of 1 to 10, perhaps she'd score a 2 on global.

Good, you will recall, includes integrity (moral, dependable, authentic) and kindness (kind, compassionate, empathetic, generous, etc.). Su Lim is courteous and nice. She smiles appropriately and treats her clients with proper respect. And because she knows her job, her clients and co-workers trust her to make the right decisions within the established parameters. She behaves ethically and, while she withholds some "truths", she would not overtly lie. She would not be described as overly generous, kind, compassionate or concerned. She demonstrates a sort of clinical empathy, but no more, which makes her appear disingenuous when she says to a client, "We care about your business." Would you score Su Lim more than a 5 or 6 on good?

If grit comprises growth, resilience, intensity and tenacity, how would you score Su Lim on the final G? She shows no appetite to learn, does only what's required to improve, does the job, but arguably sucks more energy than she pours out and is quick to find "legitimate" reasons things can't be done rather than persevering to find a way they can. Grit score? Can you score her any higher than a 3 or 4?

Su Lim scores low on 3G, and she scores low on personal ROI. Imagine if Su Lim's mindset made her truly exceptional at all the 3G qualities. If she scored at the top on all facets of global, good and grit, what happens to her personal ROI? Poor 3G Mindset, poor ROI. Strong 3G Mindset, strong ROI. 3G drives personal ROI, which drives your success.

Our discovery over the years is that there are plenty of people beyond Su Lim bursting with talent, who have all "the right stuff" but actually end up being a net *negative* to their employers because of the ways in which they drag down energy, morale, trust, loyalty, camaraderie and overall performance. Sometimes their real effect can be pretty shocking.

Take Daniel Servik (not his real name), a truly gifted actuary for one of the world's largest insurance companies. He has his PhD in mathematics from a top university and is without a doubt the fastest, most skilled and most knowledgeable at addressing actuarial problems among the entire team. He can do in his mind in half the time what most of the best do with the help of a computer. Given his special talent, any insurance executive might ask, "Where can I get one like him?" The obvious assumption would be that Daniel delivers immense value.

The reality, however, is dramatically different. The turnover among Daniel's team is *triple* the rest of the organization, and the primary reason is Daniel. When asked why they quit, Daniel's teammates describe, sometimes through tears, his monstrous ego, the way he either brutally crushes or steals everyone's ideas, his willingness to cheat or lie to get what he wants and how he constantly pits people against one another to make himself look good. As one direct report blurted, "He is simply unbearable!"

To make matters worse, Daniel is renowned for kissing up to the top bosses to win precious resources from other parts of the business that those units needed to hit their targets. He does this so he can achieve his own targets and gain more accolades. One exasperated colleague said, "He's got to be the meanest, most selfish person I've ever worked with! I swear he would sell his own mother into slavery if it would earn him a bigger bonus . . . no one, and I mean *no* one trusts that guy."

So what is Daniel's personal ROI? He solves big problems by offering big ideas and contributing concrete solutions. That represents big value for his employer. In terms of impact, he makes top talent disengage and quit and builds his "success" at the direct expense of other teams and regions. He creates a climate of distrust, stress, paranoia and fear. Daniel gets a lot of resources. He is paid handsomely, receives a full package of benefits, has a large office and generates lots of reports (many unimportant) that he expects, if not requires, dozens of other people to read. And he uses political chips to remain in power.

Is he a net positive or negative? Our simple observation is that, if an organization would breathe a collective sigh of relief if a particular person quit, then that person is probably a net negative. Even the brightest talents can generate the darkest clouds.

Likewise, at all levels of organizations we've met people of average, even below-average, talent who end up being *tremendous* net positives to their employers. They are the kind of people employers would do anything to retain, largely because of their exceptional 3G Mindsets. It makes perfect sense.

Let's assign some values. Let's say, out of 20, Daniel deserves the following scores:

$$ROI = \frac{(work + ideas + impact - resources) \times 100}{Resources}$$

Daniel's Personal ROI

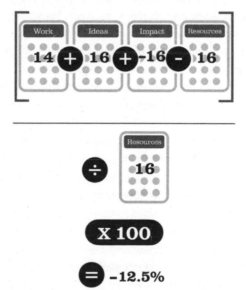

So, in Daniel's case, here's a senior guy with lots of talent whose personal ROI is significantly negative. In other words, it costs his organization more, in the fullest sense of the word, to employ him than what it gets back. And it's entirely because of Daniel's weak 3G Mindset.

A negative personal ROI is never good. It makes a powerful case for your immediate removal. A personal ROI that is marginally positive is not much better. It positions you as mediocre, and you are likely to be among the first out when your employer makes changes. It also hinders the success and momentum of those around you.

It makes perfect sense. If you agree that one of the best ways to keep a great job and flourish is to put yourself in the shoes of your employer and imagine things from their perspective, then ask yourself the question they subconsciously ask about every employee every day, "How much genuine value does that individual actually deliver to my organization?"

Knowing and, more important, optimizing this is one of the most powerful ways you can make sure that you not only get a great job but that you are then considered indispensable by anyone you work with and for. This is exactly what top employers have told us in our research: 3G drives your personal ROI. That's why employers value mindset over skill set. The right mindset creates greater value for them and for you.

You may find this next fact disturbing, or perhaps you'll find it promising: we have discovered that the people who deliver the most or the best sheer *work* are not necessarily the ones who deliver the greatest overall *value*—or become the most valued by their employers and the stakeholders, the ones who will influence their overall success at work. Value trumps work output. But how often do we assume that more work automatically means more value? The idea is to optimize the true value you bring instead of the sheer amount of work you deliver.

Think about the role your 3G Mindset plays. Beyond the obvious and observable factors, such as how much a person performs, sells, creates, assembles and delivers, what determines the net impact you have on, or the value you deliver to, the organization? We nudge employers to go beyond the normal calculations and factor in the ways in which the employee's mindset may affect morale, energy, innovation, culture, engagement, productivity and overall performance. Their conclusions, in many cases, can be surprising.

It turns out your 3G Mindset can often contribute more to personal ROI (your net value to the organization) than any other factor. Why? Because your 3G Mindset fuels every facet of who you are and what you bring to work every day.

Your goal should be to ensure that your personal ROI consistently totals more than 100 per cent because this means that the value you contribute through your work, ideas and impact will be more than double the resources you consume. When your personal ROI is consistently above 100 per cent, your contribution and value should be extremely apparent, and you will be well on your way to enjoying a flourishing career.

Minimal ROI—3G at Its Worst

For you to flourish at work through 3G, it pays to put yourself in your employer's shoes. Isn't it interesting how often business leaders come out with the clichéd comment that "Our people are our greatest asset"? And yet their management accounts typically show people as "staff costs", and people do not appear at all in either the asset or the liability sections of their company's balance sheet. The truth is that people, or certain people, are indeed their company's greatest asset, while others can be the same company's greatest liability. As you think about applying your 3G Mindset, it's good to keep that in mind.

In their day-to-day dealings, few businesspeople would agree to sign a business contract if it included a clause that exposed them to unlimited liabilities. They wouldn't want to "bet the farm" yet, strangely, they are doing so every time they hire someone. This is because an individual by his or her actions can bring a company into serious disrepute, cripple its finances and, in the most extreme instances, bring it down altogether.

This is not a hypothetical point. It is very real. The Deep Water Horizon disaster in 2010 caused unprecedented environmental damage to the Gulf of Mexico and, in doing so, cost BP billions and ruined the company's reputation. In the 1990s, the bond trader Nick Leeson's fraudulent actions single-handedly brought down Barings, one of Britain's oldest banks. And the collapse of the energy giant Enron was similarly brought about by the actions of a handful of dishonest individuals. People with major flaws in their mindsets can cause sinkholes not just in their value (personal ROI), but in their company's value.

These are a few of the most well-known examples, but there are thousands of other infamous ones. The full, extended impact of these acts is impossible to calculate but is certainly immense. Companies can be brought to their knees by negligent, incompetent or dishonest employees. You won't hear many chief executives say, "Our people are our greatest liability," but for many companies it has turned out to be true. You can use your 3G Mindset to be an exceptional asset, even when others create value craters within the organization.

Maximum ROI—3G at Its Best

At the other extreme, there are people who have enormously high personal ROIs. James recalls his first employer, Anita Roddick, the founder of the Body Shop.

"I wrote to Anita because I wanted to work for an entrepreneur. It was a long shot. And I was amazed when I got a call from her one Saturday morning. She spoke fast and with great energy and intensity. I knew immediately that I wanted to work for her. I went for an interview with Anita the following Monday. At the interview she basically listed all the things she needed to get done and then asked, 'When can you start?' My answer was, 'Immediately.'"

At this time, which was still relatively early in her career, Anita and her husband, Gordon, had built the Body Shop from nothing into a company quoted on the London Stock Exchange. Anita had also just been recognized as businesswoman of the year. She was breaking new ground. The Body Shop had made an important stand. None of the products it sold, which ranged from soaps and lotions to shampoos and cosmetics, were tested on animals. In fact, the company campaigned passionately against the testing of cosmetics on animals. Anita's business, like her, was an activist.

From its early beginnings in 1976 to Anita's untimely death in 2007, the Body Shop grew exponentially. Today, it is a global retailer with more than two thousand stores in sixty markets worldwide.

Anita really exemplified a winning 3G Mindset, and it was her 3G Mindset that powered her high personal ROI. Why? Because your 3G Mindset affects who you are and what you bring to work (and life) every day. Consider Anita through the 3G lens.

1. **Global:** Anita lifted her gaze beyond her own immediate world and scoured the planet for new products and fresh ideas. She was always on the road and on the look-out. She

shopped in the rain forests of the Amazon, the jungles of Borneo and the mountains of India for her new ideas. She was always curious about the products people of other cultures used and she adopted and blended the many good ideas she came across. The result was that she brought together an incredible range of imaginative and creative products sourced from across the planet all under the same roof and the single brand of the Body Shop.

2. **Good:** Anita built her company on an intensely ethical position. Good was not a by-product or something to keep in mind. It was at the very core of everything she did and everything she stood for, whether it was the fair trade movement for the company's suppliers, the rights of women around the world or the insistence that nothing the company sold would have been tested on animals. Her Good Mindset made her company an employer of choice, helping her attract and retain the best of the best.

3. **Grit:** Anita started her business, opening her first shop in Brighton in southern England, when her husband was on an extended assignment abroad and she was alone at home with two young daughters to look after. At a time when women entrepreneurs were a rarity and her company had little track record, she raised funds, dealt with investors and managed the regulators. This founding spirit and her great personal energy pervaded the Body Shop business as it grew. And Anita showed characteristic grit to the last, choosing to talk about her illness (hepatitis C) so that more people would understand it.

What do you think Anita's personal ROI would come in at? Pause for a moment and think about it. For although we do not have all the information we might need to calculate it precisely, we can still try. The number is clearly going to be massive. Anita was bursting with ideas, from the original concept down to the details of the product lines and how they should be merchandised. She also had a massive impact on the people she worked with and on the customers she served.

Imagine being Anita Roddick's employer, partner or co-worker. What

ROI would you assign to her? Given the immense value of her work, ideas and impact, and her genuine concern for limiting the resources she consumed, her personal ROI would clearly be hundreds, if not thousands, of per cent. Put another way, she'd be worth somewhere between ten and one hundred times what it cost to employ her.

Ask yourself, if you had twenty good people working for you, or even a hundred, whom would you promote? And how likely would you be to cut someone like Anita from your team? Or, like us, do you predict she might be the last person you'd let go? What if your employer felt the same way about you?

You don't have to be an entrepreneurial legend to achieve exceptional personal ROI. Ari Spoto is a final-year college student who runs a personal concierge service out of her rented apartment in San Luis Obispo, California, using her own car to run errands around town for her clients. She gets paid a modest hourly or daily rate but flourishes on the freedom her work provides because she can schedule it around her classes. By the nature of the job, in any given week she has several clients.

The costs of employing her are low (low resources); she always goes the extra mile to do an exceptional job, often better than the person who hired her could do (exceptional work); she constantly comes up with ingenious ways to save time and money and/or make things better (exceptional ideas); and she brings a wave of energy, cheer and genuine concern for others' happiness to all she does (exceptional impact). As a result, her personal ROI would be extremely high.

And yet you get a clear sense that Ari will deliver that level of personal ROI in anything she does. Imagine how much her clients will miss her when she graduates. Imagine how enthusiastically they will refer her to others, or serve as an effusively positive reference for her future jobs. Even as a part-time temporary employee, Ari is the kind of person you want to hire, keep, refer, reward and heap with opportunities, purely based on her personal ROI.

Your Personal ROI

Now try completing your own personal ROI calculation. Take some time and do this. It's one of the best investments you can make in your career.

Don't worry about coming up with precise numbers. It's the thought and the exercise of attempting the calculation that matters most. You can also do it online at www.3GMindset.com.

Warning and Advice: Calculating your personal ROI can be both diffi-cult and subjective. The danger is that, if this exercise is done half-heartedly, it can quickly become ineffective, rather than serving as the business-tested hard-edged tool that it is. We have used this tool to coach and guide the career success of top leaders and their people. Done right, it can create both a wake-up call and a permanent path forward to a winning, rewarding career.

Rather than relying only on your subjective self-assessment, check your assumptions with others who are best qualified to provide accurate insights. This is what we do whenever we assess our personal ROI, and it always leads to a superior result.

Again, here is the formula for determining your personal ROI:

$$ROI = \frac{(work + ideas + impact - resources) \times 100}{Resources}$$

My personal ROI calculator

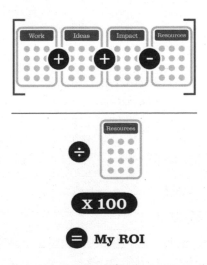

234

SCORING YOUR PERSONAL ROI—WORK, IDEAS, IMPACT

As you calculate your ROI, here are some general (unscientific) guidelines we offer to help you think about your scores for work, ideas and impact:

16 to 20: Truly Exceptional Value (top 10 per cent)

6 to 15: Well Above Average Value (upper 30 per cent)

–5 to 5: Average Value (middle 40 per cent)

–15 to –6: Well Below Average Value (lower 30 per cent)

–16 to –20 Exceptionally Low (perhaps damaging) Value (bottom 10 per cent)

WORK

What work (effort resulting in contribution) do you deliver? List all the different kinds of work (effort-based contribution) you deliver in a typical week, month or year. Does your effort enhance or detract from others? Does it enrich or deplete efficiency and effectiveness? And by how much?

_____   _____

_____   _____

_____   _____

_____   _____

_____   _____

_____   _____

_____   _____

Looking at your list, rate the overall genuine value of your work. On a scale of −20 to 20—where 20 represents the ultimate fulfilment of your complete potential to contribute at work (hint: 20 is an ideal, rarely a reality), and −20 represents the full extreme of negative, damaging effect—how would you rate your overall work? It may help to think of someone who delivers the work of many as a 20, and someone whose work has no real value but generates more low-value work for many as a −20.

IDEAS

Ideas include everything from small suggestions to major revolutions in the way people see and do things. The key element is that these are ideas that have to actually be used in some way. They have to come to life. This applies with any job, even if you are a part-time temp, because every job, including the most regimented, can be improved, and improvements generally add value. You don't have to be curing cancer for your ideas to add value.

In chapter 5, we gave you some suggestions about how to use divergent thinking and kaleidoscopic thinking to generate ideas and solutions. If it is helpful to think about and list those ideas or suggestions you have offered and seen put to use over the past week or month, or longer, you may do so below:

_____   _____
_____   _____
_____   _____
_____   _____
_____   _____
_____   _____
_____

Rate the overall value of your ideas. Using the scoring chart for guidance, on a scale of −20 to 20—where 20 represents the ultimate fulfilment of your idea potential with an immense positive impact on others and your organization, and –20 represents the full extreme of negative or damaging impact as a result of your ideas—how would you rate yours? It may help to think of those breakthroughs that drive the future or that save or make the company millions as a 20, and those ideas that take the company down a dangerous, even deadly path as a –20.

IMPACT

Impact includes all the *other* ways in which you intentionally and unintentionally affect others. This one requires exceptional insight and honesty, partially because there are so many subtle facets to impact. And partially because it's often so hard to consider the unintentionally negative ways we can affect others honestly.

Impact includes the positive or negative effect you have as a result of your style, tone, disposition, energy, words, approach, presence and behaviour. Are you extremely warm to people or colder? Are you sympathetic, empathetic and compassionate, or are you more dispassionate and distant? Do you tend to encourage or discourage? Are you welcoming and open or more removed and closed? Do you tend to add or remove energy from conversations and gatherings? Do you make people more or less effective, productive, efficient and engaged?

It may be tough for you to be a fair, objective judge of this. If in doubt, ask those who have the greatest insight and will give you the most honest answers.

_____   _____
_____   _____
_____   _____
_____   _____
_____   _____
_____   _____

Do the calculation. Rate the full positive or negative value of your impact. Using the scoring chart for guidance, on a scale of –20 to 20— where 20 represents the ultimate fulfilment of your complete impact potential with tremendous positive outcome for others, and –20 represents the full extreme of negative, even damaging effects—how would you rate your impact? Think of someone who is a human sinkhole, draining everything and everyone into the abyss as a –20. And think of someone who is the elevating, energizing soul of the company culture as a 20.

RESOURCES

Regardless of your position, it costs your organization to employ you. Probably much, much more than you imagine. When the true cost of employment is calculated for any individual in any job, it is often staggering. As a rule of thumb you can add 50 per cent to your salary, to cover the direct and indirect costs of employing you.

Resources include the comprehensive cost or value of everything provided to you by your organization. *Everything.* This includes the big, obvious things such as pay, training and benefits as well as the smaller, less obvious things such as toilet paper, light, power and space. It also includes all the time, attention and energy you demand from others. Because those have a cost too.

List the different resources you receive and/or consume to help you get a clearer sense of how your resources stack up.

_____	_____
_____	_____
_____	_____
_____	_____
_____	_____
_____	_____
_____	_____

Rate how many resources you require/use. Using the resources scoring chart for guidance, on a scale of 1 to 20, how would you rate your resources? Think of someone who gets the top pay, benefits, training, equipment and space, and demands the most time, energy and attention from others as a 20. And consider the person who works for free, provides his or her own resources (office, power, etc.) as a 1.

Score the relative and full cost of the resources required to employ you using these rough guidelines:

16 to 20: Exceptionally High Resource Cost (top 10 per cent)

10 to 15: Moderately High Resource Cost (upper 30 per cent)

5 to 10: Moderate Resource Cost (middle 60 per cent)

0 to 4: Extremely Low Resource Cost (bottom 10 per cent)

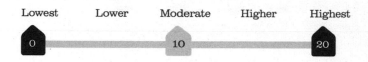

YOUR OVERALL SCORE

Now plug in your scores for work, ideas, impact and resources in the equation overleaf to determine your personal ROI.

$$ROI = \frac{(work + ideas + impact - resources) \times 100}{Resources}$$

My personal ROI calculator

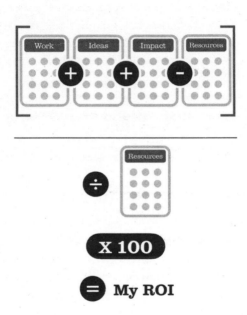

Your personal ROI will always be expressed as a percentage, so remember to multiply the number that results by 100. Clearly, the higher the number, the greater the percentage return delivered by you as an individual.

The result will be your best guess at recording your personal ROI. Now answer two questions:

1. Will your current or future employer score you similarly?
2. What do you need to do to substantially (and relentlessly) improve your score?

The results from the personal ROI calculation can fall into an extraordinarily broad range. If you were to run this calculation, or do this exercise repeatedly, applied to a broad range of people, it would be impossible not to come to this conclusion: one person can make a tremendous (positive or negative) difference, and the chasm between a "good" hire and a "bad" one can be truly massive.

Although personal ROI can be calculated, it's much more about the principle than about the number. It's about being obsessed with optimizing the genuine net value you bring to everyone you work with and for, and to your organization overall. You may find it tough to come up with exact numbers on each component, but that's okay. The idea is to think about where you are now and how you can strengthen your overall personal ROI. Again, consider how your 3G Mindset pervades the entire formula.

Growing Your Career the 3G Way— The Employers' Perspective

Of all the ideas, tools, models and concepts we offer to employers worldwide, no other tool resonates as strongly or generates more excitement than combining 3G Mindset with personal ROI. Employers instantly "get it", citing the 3G–personal ROI combination as the explanation they have long been looking for as to why they have made so many of the decisions about whom they hire, promote, value, keep and want to grow. And nearly every employer we interview has a "3G drives value" (personal ROI) story to tell about someone.

Given the tools and knowledge you have gained, we see no reason why your next employer shouldn't tell a glowing "3G Mindset drives personal ROI" story about you as you *Put Your Mindset to Work*. Consider the following two examples (among countless others) to spark your imagination as you ask yourself, "What do I want my current (or next) employer to say about *me*?"

THE REAL STORIES—MINDSET

Carol Urick, a vice president at a large insurance company, tells the story of a young woman (who, Carol said, is too modest to have us mention her name) she had met while working at a former role in the investment banking world. The young woman, through sheer willpower and determination, carved her own future in life. She was working in a "backroom banking job" on the night shift sorting payments. This young woman had made it clear that she wanted desperately to do something more with her life. "It was her mindset, not her skill set, that won us over. Believe me."

Initially, the young woman was seeking a sales associate's job (mostly clerical), and she worked like mad to get it. Eventually, thanks to her amazing mindset, she worked her way up to support a broker in one of the bank branches. She wanted to continue to move her career forward and spent much time identifying what she would need to do to transition to the broker role. This young woman had some challenges when it came to studying. It was the kind of thing that could have been a deal breaker for her, since much of what lay ahead required studying for and passing many licences.

Most people would have given up. Not her. She just worked harder. She took the same exam over and over, and gave it her all. After successfully passing it, she was provided a role in a bank branch as a junior broker, then eventually became a full-fledged broker. She quickly became rookie of the year. She's so exceptional. She's tenacious, empathetic, authentic, honest and really curious about all the people that she is now empowered to assist. She's a good person with tremendous grit, and she gets the big picture.

Here's a woman who many may have felt was unimpressive on paper. But her mindset—all the things we mentioned above, plus her tremendous persistence, growth and hunger to learn—made her one of the region's most prized people over many others with far greater qualifications and experience on paper. Carol told us, "I felt then that she had a very bright future and she indeed has proved that since! We have all moved to new programmes since that time, however, but I stayed in touch. She continues to be impressive in her career achievements and has found great success and happiness."

Here's another industry leader's perspective.

According to Steve Collins, Mars, Inc.'s global chocolate leader for the world's biggest customer, Walmart, "When it comes to driving the greatest value for the business, I'd pick the person with the right mindset, any day."

When asked to name names, he said, "I've got some great people. But Jim Dodge is a guy working for me who wakes up every day asking himself, 'How can I be better? How am I going to amaze myself and others with what I'm about to do?'"

Steve doesn't hold back on linking mindset to tangible value. "One guy like that is worth five or more 'normal' people. Jim, and the others like him who have that winning mindset, are driving the future of our business. Those are the folks we want to keep, long term."

Putting your 3G Mindset to work and seeking to maximize your personal ROI is a great way to ensure that you relentlessly grow in both your current and your future roles. It can help you leapfrog over other far more qualified candidates.

It's a brutal truth. People often forget (and easily cut or fail to promote) the Su Lims of the world, who put in the long hours but lack the mindset to deliver the personal ROI that would make them special.

Ari Spoto, Jim Dodge, Anita Roddick—and the people the world's top employers talk about—prove that, regardless of where you are in your career, you can apply all the facets of your 3G Mindset to optimize all the facets of your personal ROI. And, when you do, you dramatically increase the chances that you become the most readily promoted, most stubbornly retained and most prized member of your workforce, resulting in an uncommonly successful and rewarding career.

And that is precisely our heartfelt aspiration for you.

This chapter has suggested how you can best apply your new and improved 3G Mindset to keep, then advance and flourish within the best jobs.

CHAPTER RECAP
3G →Personal ROI →Success at Work

Personal ROI Formula

$$ROI = \frac{(work + ideas + impact - resources) \times 100}{Resources}$$

Personal ROI is the most powerful way to put your 3G Mindset to work.

Use your 3G Mindset to optimize your Personal ROI every day, and you will become one of the most sought after, prized and rewarded employees, being offered the kind of responsibilities and opportunities few others earn or enjoy.

Conclusion

We began this book and this journey—and perhaps you did too—with this question: "What is the one thing that could most dramatically enhance my chances of getting, keeping and flourishing in the best jobs?"

You and the people you hope to work with provide the same answer and clarifier: your mindset. But not just *any* mindset.

You now know that the ideal or winning mindset is the 3G Mindset. That's what the best science and the world's top employers are telling you, in utter harmony. You understand that having a lens forged with a strong blend of global, good and grit sets you apart and makes you the kind of person employers desperately want to hire, promote, retain and find more of.

As a member of Gen G, or Generation Global, you have stiffer competition and a broader array of opportunities than any generation at any time in history. This is a whole new era, like in an epic flood where all walls have been demolished. Whether that makes you wither or flourish is entirely determined by that same thing: your 3G Mindset. Never has this mattered more than it does now.

3G is not a magic pill you take to be instantly transformed. It is a timeless path, a personal and elevating quest to which you commit to become an ever better person and to enjoy an ever richer life.

This relates to our opening promise to you: "to multiply your chances of enjoying uncommon success at work, while enriching your life immensely along the way". Beyond the focus of our work-related examples, we hope you have been privately applying every principle and tool to all the other facets of your life. Because, as you have no doubt figured out, everything within these pages applies with equal power and promise to your world beyond work.

This book has been focused on work. We chose work because we care immensely about human dignity, your dignity, your sense of significance—the sense that who you are and what you do matters—that can be uniquely fed by work. We chose work because we share a common passion for seeing people truly flourish in their pursuits.

We also care deeply about personal energy. Because, without energy, without that inner life force, it's tough to pursue, achieve, contribute and enjoy much of anything. Work, mindset and energy share a powerful relationship.

Through this research, we asked more than 500,000 people worldwide these three questions:

1. What do you consider to be the prime energy years of a contributing human being's life?
2. What do you consider to be the prime energy days of the week?
3. What are the prime energy hours of the week?

How would you answer them? Here are their answers. Roughly 90 per cent said:

1. The prime energy years of a contributing human being's life are twenty-five to fifty-five years old.
2. The prime energy days of the week are Monday through Thursday.
3. The prime energy hours of the week are 7 a.m. to 3 p.m.

This means that, if you're lucky enough to have a job, you will spend a significant chunk of your prime energy hours of life *at work*. And that means that sacrificing the prime energy hours of your life by doing something you hate or dread now in order to buy free but reduced energy hours later is a poor strategy.

Ideally, you will create a working life that is rewarding, enriching and energizing. We wish for you that feeling of immense gratification that comes when you achieve exceptional personal ROI in all that you do. And we know no better way to achieve this than to wake up each day, and *Put Your Mindset to Work*.

> Work is life, you know, and without it, there's nothing but fear and insecurity.
>
> *– John Lennon*

ACKNOWLEDGEMENTS

We wish to acknowledge and express our heartfelt gratitude to everyone who helped make *Put Your Mindset to Work* a reality. Specifically, we wish to thank the thousands of employers who participated in our research over the years, the world of top-flight scholars who offered their time and wisdom to enrich our understanding and approach, and our valued colleagues whose frank feedback and insights made us and our work so much better.

We particularly want to thank the REED Team (Sarah Reynolds, Katy Nicholson, Marc Harris, Heidi Cross, Martin Warnes, Giulia Bertolini, and dozens more); the PEAK Team (Tina Miller, Jeff Thompson, Katie Martin, Steve Cohen); Dr Jerilee Grandy for her psychometric brilliance; and many more. We especially want to thank our beloved (and patient) spouses and families for sacrificing so much and making this more of a quest than a mere book. We hope we have done you proud.

Jill Marsal, our agent, was an exemplar of 3G in bringing this book from concept to reality. This book is a tribute to you and your rare, values-based approach to bringing the best work to the world. We are better authors thanks to you. You are truly exceptional.

We thank our prized editor, Courtney Young, as well as Adrian Zackheim, esteemed founder of Portfolio. Thank you for seeing the potential.

Finally, we thank you, our reader, for having the desire and courage to make work more than a job. We applaud your heartfelt effort to *Put Your Mindset to Work*.

NOTES

1   **Triple your chances of getting and keeping the best job** Based on an independent study of 30,000 unsuccessful versus successful CVs (see p. 195).

1   **in the eyes of your boss or key stakeholders** According to a study we conducted with top employers (see p. 18).

3   **And there are some landmark studies that prove it.** For more information on AQ-related findings and research, go to www. peaklearning.com.

8   **and drives a *lot* of factors, including how much money you make.** Based on a series of 2010 independent studies, beginning with the initial analysis of the results of 895 3G Panorama respondents conducted in 2010 by senior researcher and psychometrician Dr Jerilee Grandy.

CHAPTER ONE: THE NEW REALITY – WHAT EMPLOYERS REALLY WANT

14   **the most ADD-as-normal age group in human history.** Clay Shirky, *Cognitive Surplus: Creativity and Generosity in a Connected Age* (New York: Penguin Press, 2010).

18   **"a commitment to creating search perfection and having a great time doing it".** www.google.com/intl/en/corporate/culture.html.

18   **a person with the right mindset is seven times more valuable** Each employer was asked the same question, then asked to quantify his or her response by answering, "Specifically, how many 'normal' employees would you trade for one person with the right mindset?" The response scores ranged from 3 to 10, with a mean of 7.2.

_____

CHAPTER TWO: THE WINNING MINDSET – INTRODUCING 3G

29 **predicts how much money you tend to make.** Based on a series of 2010 independent studies, beginning with the initial analysis of the results of 895 3G Panorama respondents conducted in 2010 by senior researcher and psychometrician Dr Jerilee Grandy.

29 **"You cannot fulfil your career potential without a global mindset."** Personal interview with Dr Stephen L. Cohen conducted by Dr Paul G. Stoltz, 2010.

29 **a diverse group of human resources executives in two hundred global organizations.** Marshall Goldsmith, Alastair Robertson, Cathy Greenberg and Maya Hu-Chan, *Global Leadership: The Next Generation* (New Jersey: FT Press, 2003).

31 **determines how you as a leader are rated and valued by others.** Michael E. Brown, Linda K. Trevino and David A. Harrison, "Ethical Leadership: A Social Learning Perspective for Construct Development and Testing", *Organizational Behaviour and Human Decision Processes* 97, no. 2 (2005): 117–34.

31 **on your commitment level and likelihood to quit.** Kathryn M. Bartol, "Professionalism as a Predictor of Organizational Commitment, Role Stress and Turnover: A Multidimensional Approach", *Academy of Management Journal* 22, no. 4 (1979): 815–21.

41 **invented a new word to describe this phenomenon. He called it "co-opetition".** Adam M. Brandenburger and Barry J. Nalebuff, *Co-opetition: A Revolutionary Mindset That Combines Competition and Co-operation: The Game Theory Strategy That's Changing the Game of Business* (New York: Currency, 1996).

_____

CHAPTER THREE: MEASURE YOUR MINDSET – THE 3G PANORAMA

60 **whose mindset feeds the belief "I can do better if I apply myself."** Carol S. Dweck, *Mindset: The New Psychology of Success* (New York: Random House, 2006).

62 **in his book *The Shallows*** Nicholas Carr, *The Shallows: How the Internet is Changing the Way We Think, Read and Remember* (New York: W. W. Norton, 2010).

65 **is listed as one of the fifty worst jobs in the United States.** *Wall Street Journal*, http://online.wsj.com/public/resources/documents/st_BESTJOBS2010_20100105.html, 5 January 2010.

CHAPTER FOUR: MASTER YOUR MINDSET – HOW IT ALL WORKS

75 **"creates the biochemical change in the brain to take you forward".** K. Anders Ericsson, Ralf Krampe and Clemens Tesch-Römer, "The Role of Deliberate Practice in the Acquisition of Expert Performance", *Psychological Review* 100, no. 3 (1993): 363–406.

77 **Cabbies just go on acquiring even more brain capacity as they gain more experience.** Eleanor A. Maguire et al., "Navigation-related Structural Change in the Hippocampi of Taxi Drivers", *PNAS* 97, no. 8 (11 April 2000): 4398–403.

77 **actually changes the brain's internal function and structures.** Richard J. Davidson and Antoine Lutz, "Buddha's Brain: Neuroplasticity and Meditation", *IEEE Signal Processing Magazine* (January 2008).

78 **appear to be at least partially, even significantly, genetic.** Martin E. P. Seligman, *Learned Optimism: How to Change Your Mind and Your Life* (New York: Alfred A. Knopf, 1991).

78 **directly inherited through unchangeable genes.** David Shenk, *The Genius in All of Us: Why Everything You've Been Told About Genetics, Talent and Intelligence is Wrong* (New York: Doubleday, 2010): 14, quoting the conclusions of *The Bell Curve* (1994) by Richard Herrnstein and Charles Murray as "quite mistaken" and contrasting these with quotes from world authority on genes and development Michael Meaney, from McGill University.

78 **as author David Shenk has explained,** ibid.

79 **"genes multiplied by environment" (G × E),** ibid., 26–8.

79 **environmentally induced changes can actually be inherited.** Ibid., 131–2 on epigenetics. In 1999, botanist Enrico Coen and colleagues at the United Kingdom's John Innes Centre tried to isolate the genetic differences between two distinct types of the toadflax plant . . . The difference couldn't be found in the genes, which were identical, but in the epigenome (the protective packaging of historic proteins that protect the DNA and keep it compact and also serve as a mediator for gene expression). Enrico discovered that these alterations can

be inherited, and Australian geneticists Daniel Morgan and Emma Whitelaw made similar discoveries about mice. On p. 132, Shenk lists four scientific papers published between 2004 and 2007 confirming the inherited nature of such environmentally caused epigenetic changes.

80 **Dweck's growth dimension is a vital component of both your grit and your overall 3G Mindset.** Carol S. Dweck, *Mindset: The New Psychology of Success* (New York: Random House, 2006).

81 **the brain impact of copying angry expressions was drastically reduced.** Andreas Hennenlotte et al., "The Link between Facial Feedback and Neural Activity within Central Circuitries of Emotion—New Insights from Botulinum Toxin-Induced Denervation of Frown Muscles", *Cerebral Cortex* 19, no. 3 (June 2008): 537–42.

81 **mirror neurons help explain how empathy works.** Jean-Pierre P. Changeux, Antonio Damasio and Wolf J. Singer, *Neurobiology of Human Values (Research and Perspectives in Neurosciences)*, (New York: Springer-Verlag Berlin Heidelberg, 2005), 107–23.

82 **famous Stanford Prison Experiment in 1971.** Philip Zimbardo, *The Lucifer Effect: How Good People Turn Evil* (New York: Random House, 2007). Zimbardo randomly assigned ordinary Harvard students to take on the roles of guards or prisoners. Within just a few hours the "prisoners" slumped into passive despair, while the guards became increasingly bullying and "creatively evil".

83 **"no man is an island, entire of itself"** John Donne, *Devotions upon Emergent Occasion and Death's Duel* (New York: Random House, 1999).

83 **a support group of other people on the same path.** Nicholas A. Christakis and James H. Fowler, *Connected: The Surprising Power of Our Social Networks and How They Shape Our Lives* (New York: Little, Brown and Company, 2009): 130, quotes study showing that weight loss is 33 per cent greater and more durable when people are part of a group (R. R. Wing and R. W. Jeffrey, "Benefits of Recruiting Participants with Friends and Increasing Social Support for Weight Loss and Maintenance", *Journal of Consulting and Classical Psychology* 67 [1999]: 132–8).

84 **a very personal story about how this worked for him.** Dan Ariely, *The Upside of Irrationality: The Unexpected Benefits of Defying Logic at Work and at Home* (New York: Harper Collins, 2010): 1–5.

85 **"big-bonus group performed worst of all"**. Dan Ariely, "Bonuses Boost Activity, Not Quality", *Wired Magazine* 1 (February 2010); also see Ariely, *The Upside of Irrationality*, 21–38.

85 **"derive pleasure from doing so"**. Samuel Bowles and Sandra Polania Reyes, "Economic Incentives and Social Preferences: A Preference-Based Lucas Critique of Public Policy", CESifo Working Paper Series No. 2734, CESifo Group Munich, 2009, launched at the LSE, London, UK, in June 2009, www2.lse.ac.uk/newsAndMedia/news/archives/2009/06/performancepay.aspx.

86 **"without concern for external rewards, spontaneously and with full commitment"**. Mihaly Csikszentmihalyi and Isabella Selega Csikszentmihalyi, eds., *Optimal Experience: Psychological Studies of Flow in Consciousness* (Cambridge: Cambridge University Press, 1992). Note that Csikszentmihalyi's term *yu* is also known as the Taoist principal of wu-wei.

87 **outperformed the short-term committed by an astonishing 400 per cent.** Daniel Coyle, *The Talent Code: Greatness isn't Born It's Grown* (London: Random House, 2009): 104; see Gary McPherson "From Child to Musician: Skill Development During the Beginning Stages of Learning an Instrument", *Psychology of Music* (January 2005).

87–8 **to see how completely many of the classic rewards can backfire** Daniel H. Pink, *Drive: The Surprising Truth about What Motivates Us* (New York: Riverhead Books, 2009): 72; Edward Deci and Richard Ryan, behavioural scientists based at the University of Rochester in New York, have established a network of Self-Determination Theory (SDT) scholars throughout the United States, Canada, Israel, Singapore and western Europe, exploring self-determination and intrinsic motivation through hundreds of research papers. Other leaders in this field include economists Roland Benabou of Princeton University, Bruno Frey of University of Zurich, Harvard University's Howard Gardner and Tufts University's Robert Sternberg. Pink's three elements of intrinsic motivation, autonomy, mastery and purpose (85–146) underpin the analysis given here.

CHAPTER FIVE: GROW YOUR MINDSET – GLOBAL

100 **"It is now 'Think and act both globally and locally'"** Dr Stephen L. Cohen, "Global Leadership Requires a Global Mindset", *Industrial and Commercial Training* 42, no. 1 (2001): 3–10, Emerald Group Publishing

Ltd. www.strategicleadershipcollaborative.com/articles/Stephen_L_ Cohen.pdf.

105 **the little subgroup we rely on for support when disputes break out.** Robin Dunbar, *Grooming, Gossip and the Evolution of Language* (Cambridge: Harvard University Press, 1997); Robin Dunbar and Susanne Shultz, "Evolution in the Social Brain", *Science* 317, no. 5843 (7 September 2007): 1344–7.

105 **the same two to five on the ground floor. The image below depicts this.** Motivation: Social Brain Theory diagram reprinted with permission from Professor Alistair Sutcliffe and the University of Manchester.

113 **According to Harvard and University of California scientists Nicholas Christakis and James Fowler** Nicholas A. Christakis and James H. Fowler, *Connected: The Surprising Power of our Social Networks and How They Shape Our Lives* (New York: Little, Brown and Company, 2009): 50–4.

113 **Each unhappy friend decreases it by 7 per cent.** Ibid., 51–2.

115 **to help their future working life than any other non-work activity.** According to a survey carried out among 1,450 job seekers by reed.co.uk, "The Impact of Voluntary/Charity Sector Involvement", September 2010.

123 **a theory that psychologist Liam Hudson had come up with in 1966.** Liam Hudson, *Contrary Imaginations: A Psychological Study of the English Schoolboy* (Harmondsworth, UK: Penguin, 1967).

CHAPTER SIX: GROW YOUR MINDSET – GOOD

132 **superior engagement of their people. Good creates good.** Michael Brown, Linda K. Trevino and David A. Harrison, "Ethical Leadership: A Social Learning Perspective for Construct Development and Testing", *Organizational Behaviour and Human Decision Processes* 97, no. 2 (2005).

134 **factors ethical and environmental matters into their purchasing decisions these days** Concerned Consumer Index, monthly poll by Good Business/Populus, 2010: "Currently around half of all adult consumers factor ethical considerations into their purchasing decisions"; www.populus.co.uk/concerned-consumer-index-230810.html.

135 **"great people, decency, thoughtfulness and attentive listening".** Tom Peters, "Kindness Can Be the Hardest Word of All", *Financial Times*, 24 August 2010.

135 **"My observation: Kind works! And pays off!"** Ibid.

153 **when they essentially paid students to cheat on a test.** Nina Mazar, On Amir and Dan Ariely, "The Dishonesty of Honest People: A Theory of Self-Concept Maintenance", *Journal of Marketing Research* XLV (December 2008), 633–44.

154 **Likewise, a study by Joseph Henrich at the University of British Columbia** Joseph Henrich et al., "Markets, Religion, Community Size and the Evolution of Fairness and Punishment", *Science* 327, no. 5972 (19 March 2010), 1480–4. "The Origins of Selfishness", *The Economist* (18 March 2010), says "Dr Henrich . . . found that the sense of fairness in a society was linked to the degree of its participation in a world religion."

CHAPTER SEVEN: GROW YOUR MINDSET – GRIT

167 **and that one can always do better, are far more likely to up their game.** Carol S. Dweck, *Mindset: The New Psychology of Success* (New York: Random House, 2006).

171 **Paul's three Adversity Quotient (AQ)-related books.** Dr Paul G. Stoltz with Erik Weihenmayer, *Adversity Quotient: Turning Obstacles into Opportunities* (New York: Wiley, 1997); Dr Paul G. Stoltz, *The Adversity Advantage: Turning Everyday Struggles into Everyday Greatness* (New York: Fireside, 2007); Dr Paul G. Stoltz, *The Adversity Quotient at Work: Make Everyday Challenges the Key to Your Success—Putting the Principles of AQ into Action* (New York: William Morrow, 2000).

177 **diagnosed levels of ADHD (attention deficit/hyperactivity disorder)** ADHD is a problem with inattentiveness, overactivity, impulsivity, or a combination. Definition from www.nlm.nih.gov/ medlineplus/ency/article/001551.htm.

177 **have tripled worldwide.** Eric Taylor et al., "Attention Deficit Hyperactivity Disorder: Diagnosis and management of ADHD in children, young people and adults", *NICE* (September 2008), www. nice.org.uk/nicemedia/pdf/CG72FullGuideline.pdf.

177 **Worldwide consumption of television is now over one trillion hours every year.** Clay Shirky, *Cognitive Surplus: Creativity and Generosity in a Connected Age* (New York: Penguin Press, 2010).

177 **teenage vocabulary has dropped by half compared to the 1950s.** Report to the Board of School Trustees, Metropolitan School District of Mortinsville, 2001, http://msdadmin.scican.net/minutes/board%20 minutes/2001/brd71701.htm.

177 **an average daily exposure of just under eleven hours of electronic media.** Quoted by Hal Crowther in "100 Fears of Solitude", *The Daily Telegraph*, 13 August 2010, first published in *Granta* III.

178 **new neural pathways in our brains while weakening old ones.** Gary Small and Gigi Borgan, *iBrain: Surviving the Technological Alternation of the Modern Mind* (New York: HarperCollins, 2008).

178 **dozens of studies from psychologists, neurobiologists, educators and web designers that point to the same conclusion:** Nicholas Carr, *The Shallows: How the Internet is Changing the Way We Think, Read and Remember* (New York: W. W. Norton, 2010).

178 **"promotes cursory reading, hurried and distracted thinking and superficial learning".** Ibid.

178 **people spend between nineteen and twenty-seven seconds looking at a page of internet information before moving on.** "Puzzling Web Habits Across the Globe", Click Tales blog, 31 July 2008, http://blog.clicktale.com/2008/07/31/puzzling-web-habits-across-the-globe-part-1.

178 **"less deliberative . . . less able to think and reason out a problem".** Quoted in Don Tapscott, *Grown Up Digital* (New York: McGraw Hill, 2009): 108–9.

178 **by psychologist Dr Glenn Wilson, funded by Hewlett-Packard.** Michael Horsnell, "Why Texting Harms Your IQ", *The Sunday Times*, 22 April 2005.

179 **"a mythical activity in which people believe they can perform two or more tasks simultaneously".** Edward Hallowell, *CrazyBusy: Overstretched, Overbooked and About to Snap! Strategies for Handling Your Fast-Paced Life* (New York: Ballantine Books, 2007).

179 **worse than driving while intoxicated.** Helen Nugent, "Texting While Driving is More Dangerous Than Drink-Driving," *The Times*, 18 September 2008, reporting Transport Research Laboratory research commissioned by the RAC Foundation.

180 **"symptoms of a weak and frivolous mind".** Philip Stanhope, *Letters to His Son* (London: J. Dodsley, 1774), Letter CXXI.

180 **"owing more to patient attention than to any other talent".** Quoted in Christine Rosen, "The Myth of Multitasking", *The New Atlantis* 105 (Spring 2008).

180 **answering e-mails or texts to return to their original task.**
Gloria Mark et al., "No Task Left Behind? Examining the Nature of
Fragmented Work", paper written for and presented at the Computer-
Human Interaction Conference (CHI) 2005, 2–7 April 2005, Portland,
Oregon: http://portal.acm.org/citation.cfm?id=1055017.

180 **costs the US economy $650 billion a year in lost productivity.**
Quoted by Steve Lohr, "Slow Down Brave Multi-Tasker, and Don't
Read This in Traffic", *New York Times*, 25 March 2007.

180 **René Marois of Vanderbilt University used fMRI scans** Functional
magnetic resonance imaging scans are an advanced method of
neuro-imaging.

180 **as the brain determines which task to perform.** René Marois et al.,
"Isolation of a Central Bottleneck of Information Processing with Time
Resolved fMRI", *Neuron* 52, no. 6 (21 December 2006): 1109–20.

180 **an American study reported in the *Journal of Experimental
Psychology*.** Joshua S. Rubinstein, David E. Meyer and Jeffrey E. Evans,
"Executive Control of Cognitive Processes in Task Switching", *Journal
of Experimental Psychology: Human Perception and Performance* 27, no. 4,
763–97.

181 **limits how much you can retrieve and use.** Kevin Foerde, Barbara
J. Knowlton and Russell A. Poldrack, "Modulation of Competing
Memory Systems by Distraction", *PNAS* 103, no. 31 (1 August 2006),
11778–83.

181 **"humans are not built to work this way. We're really built to
focus."** Quoted in Christine Rosen, "The Myth of Multitasking", *The
New Atlantis* 105 (Spring 2008).

181 **can be learned, even mastered.** Mihaly Csikszentmihalyi. *Flow: The
Psychology of Optimal Experience* (New York: HarperCollins, 2008).

181 **"with the feeling I get when I am out sailing".** Ibid., 67.

CHAPTER EIGHT: GET THE BEST JOBS, THE 3G WAY

194 **The Winning CV Study.** Thirty thousand CVs, filtered to
represent the total sample of appropriate/good quality responses
to specific advertised vacancies, were analysed for this study.
The CV sample was chosen to be representative of response across
different time frames (from 2007 to 2010) and in different job sectors

(including accountancy, administration, IT, education, financial and health roles). Research methodology included use of key-word-searching computer software as well as an independent research team applying standardized criteria to record a series of characteristics and traits in each. CVs were divided into three categories so that similarities and differences between them could be reported on according to outcome. CVs of individuals who gained the job (the "winning" CV) were compared against short-listed CVs as well as those that were not selected to progress (the "losing" CV). See 3GMindset.com for a complete description of the winning CV study.

CONCLUSION

249 **there's nothing but fear and insecurity.** Geoffrey Giuliano, *Lennon in America, 1971–1980* (New York: Cooper Square Press, 2000).

INDEX